My Life as a Psychic Medium

Walking In Two Worlds

Donna J. Hayes

MY LIFE AS A PSYCHIC MEDIUM

By Donna J. Hayes

Edited by Stacy R. Webb

Backintyme Publishing

978-0-939479-64-1

Acknowledgments

This book is dedicated to Detective Bob Lyles (retired) of the Hopkinsville Police Department. For all his help and open-mindedness. This book may not have come about without your help in understanding.

I would also like to say thank you to my friends and family. For putting up with me. While I know having me in your life hasn't been easy. Your understanding and loyalty have been appreciated beyond words.

Table of Contents

My Abilities

The Body

The human body is a complex being. It works daily without our even being aware of it. We take for granted that it is going to continue doing its job without any help from us.

Being able to look inside someone's body and see what is going on is something that still amazes me. I can look at you and see inside your body as if it were made of glass.

How I do this? I do not know. Edgar Cayce, a native of Hopkinsville, Kentucky was known as the Sleeping Prophet. He used this ability to help thousands. It was only one of the many talents he was known for. This is what is known as "Psychic Diagnostician". He would lie down on his couch and go into a trance, during which his spirit would leave his body. His spirit would then travel to where the person he was to read. He would look inside their body, and diagnose what illness or injury, and then he would proceed to instruct them on how to correct the problem.

Edgar Cayce, like me, never knew where his gift came from. He, as well as I, believed that it is a gift from God, and meant to be utilized to help others. At his death, his body was returned to Kentucky for burial at Riverside Cemetery here in Hopkinsville, Ky.

What I do runs along the same lines as what he did in his lifetime, only I do it while I am awake. First let me state that I am not a doctor. I cannot diagnose an illness, nor do I have a medical degree. When I do readings for someone who asks about their health, I look inside their body to see what I can pick up. If I do see something, I tell them, "That they need to see a doctor, and I let them know in which area I think the doctor should look.

How I can do this, I do not know. Other than what I know of Edgar Cayce, and what he did, I have never found anyone else that can do it. I have heard of people being able to do something similar, but not the exact same thing. I also have never found anyone that can explain to me how or why this ability works.

I have met and talked to local doctors, many of whose patients are my clients. They have explained to me that I have been right many times, but not every time. I am correct about 90% of the time, and I usually am in the right area where the trouble is found. The first thing I do when asked to do this is to look at the outside of the body. I do not ask anyone to remove his clothes because this is not necessary. I can pick up anything in the body underneath clothing. I have learned that different colors tell me about different diseases. Most of the time, these colors radiate from inside the body, not the outside.

When I look at the body, I see the same physical characteristics other people see. I then close everything off around me to get a closer look at the inside of the body. I see the bone structure as you would if you were looking at an x-ray. The only way I can explain this is to say most of us have seen a skeleton or pictures of one hanging in the doctor's office. It shows the bone structure as if you had removed the outer layer from the body and left the bones bare. This is what I see when I get a closer look.

I can see hairline cracks where bones have been broken in the past, and how they have healed. I can see if they have not healed properly and if this could be the problem causing the pain. I see the joints as they move, and if they are fitted properly together.

I have found out that often when I see the bones, there are different images I pick up from them as well. One of the things I pick up most is a white powder looking substance around the joints. It looks like baby powder. People have told me that this is where they have a lot of pain. In addition, it hurts when they move it. I feel that what I am seeing is inflammation or deposits of some kind in the joints, and they may need to have this area looked at.

Another color I pick up is a very strong green coming from inside the bones. I have found that this color lets me visualize what I believe to be cancer. The reason I say this is that when reading for people who have subsequently been diagnosed by their doctor as having cancer, I have picked up the same colors and feelings.

Sometimes I pick up a dull gray color for the marrow inside the bone, I do not know what this color is telling me or what diseases it is showing me, because I have seen it in so few people. I can also tell if there is something wrong with the bone marrow because of the color change in it. The coloring can be different, or I pick up spots in the gray. What this means I really do not know, but I tell people that they really do need to see a doctor soon about this. The reason for this is that when I pick this up, I get a very bad feeling along with it.

First, I look at the internal organs. I can see inside them and tell when they are not working properly as they should. This way I can tell by the beating of the heart if I have gone deep enough. I can see the blood pumping through the heart, and I can tell when something is blocking the heart or the arteries. I can see the heart valves as they open and close, or if they are blocked. I can do this with all parts of the body and know if they are functioning properly.

I can see tumors that are attached to different parts of the body. I can tell if the tumor is cancerous if I see a green color. If not, they look to be black in color and are normal. I can distinguish tumors on the inside of a woman's breasts, or if it is just milk ducts that are affected. I can see the female organs, such as the uterus, fallopian tubes and ovaries, and tell if there is anything wrong with them. I can see all parts of the body such as kidneys, spleen, intestine, and colon. I can see muscle tissue and tell if it is inflamed or pulled. I view the inside and out of the body as if it were on an operating table ready for surgery.

The one part of the body that I can look inside of that surprises me even to this day is the brain, I first look at the (skull) and can tell if you have had a concussion by any cracks I see there, from past or present, or if there is a place that has not healed properly. Then as I look deeper, I can see what might look like a road map to most people if they were to view it. I can see the nerves as they work, and I can see the little veins and arteries as they pump blood through the brain. I can tell when they are not getting a good blood supply going into them, if there is a faulty connection, or if they just do not function at all. I can also see if parts of the brain have shut down, and most of the time I can see why. I can see tumors on the brain that bar the blood flow, or if there is a place that is not getting any blood flow at all.

I know you are asking "Can she really accomplish all of this by just looking at someone?" If so, then why isn't she helping people?" I would, given, the opportunity. It is just that no one has fully studied this realm of psychic ability, and it is not easy to find someone much less convince a physician to diagnose a patient based on my diagnosis. No one will lay his or her reputation and license on the line to do this study in finding out how it works. I would love to know how I do this, because I have lived with these abilities for years.

I do know that this is one of my abilities that does not drain me mentally as well as physically. Most of the others, if I do them daily, drain me to the point that I must sleep to recharge my energy. People do not realize that you are using a part of your brain that is not normally used. To work this part of the brain takes tremendous effort and time using it. I know when to stop when I get to the point, I am mentally exhausted. I must shut down my brain and put a wall up to block out everything going on around me just to be able to function in the normal world; you could not by any means call this or any part of my life normal.

Minds

One of the hardest abilities I deal with is the ability to read minds. This is what is known as ESP. I call it irritating and worrisome. I do not do it all the time; it happens mostly when I am not concentrating on keeping others' thoughts out. I am a stickler for privacy, and to do this goes against my beliefs. I can walk by someone, pick up thoughts running through his or her mind, and get a mental picture of what he is thinking. I can do it if I feel there is a need, as when I work on a murder case. My children do not care for it, but they know better than to lie to me. I have caught myself doing this when I do not really mean to. Knowing other people's thoughts is not always good. I notice what people think about me, and sometimes I do not like what I hear. The old saying about a person eavesdropping on other people's conversations is very true. You never hear anything good about yourself.

It helps a great deal when I am working on a murder case. I have been asked to go into courtrooms to do this with someone the police feel is a danger to other people. Sometimes I just get fragments of what is going on in their minds, but most of the time I can pick up their entire train of thought. I have had district attorneys ask me to do this, in murder cases. Nothing I say can be used in court; but I do this to give them directions on where to go with questioning. They are hoping the murderer will trip himself up, implicating himself by his answers.

Touch

Touch is one of the five senses we use every day of our lives, and never think anything about. You may pick up objects a hundred times a day, without thinking about it. When I pick up an object, it is different. I also perceive feelings and emotions from the people who have owned it. I see pictures of happenings in their lives, as well as pictures of them. I must stop myself from letting everything come through to me.

People often use this to test my abilities. They hand me an object and say, "Tell me about the person who owned it." There have been instances that I cannot pick up anything from an object, but not often. Most of the time, it is something about the person in the family who is deceased. I tell them about the emotions and characteristics of the person or maybe the location where the object has been. I tell them what the person looks like that I pick up. They usually can identify the person from the description I give them.

I try to close my mind off from this happening, because most people do not want you to know information about them without their telling you. I try not to use this as a way to get into others' lives. Every one of us has secrets in our lives that only we should know, moments in time we hold dear to our hearts.

To use this ability, I hold an object in my hand or just touch it with my fingertips. At times I pick up pain coming from the person that owns it. The feeling I get is hard to describe; it's like bumping your hand on something and not seeing anything visible on the outside to explain the feeling you are experiencing, but you know the pain is real, just deep inside your head. This is the sensation that I feel. I pick up happiness as well as pain.

I can do this with just about any object you bring to me. I have even had people bring me something from an animal that they have lost, hoping that I can help them get their babies back. I am an animal lover and do not charge for this. If it were my dog or cat, I would want help from anywhere I could get it. Sometimes I am lucky and know if they are alive and if they will be back with them soon.

I love going to stock car races whenever I can. I have dated mechanics that have worked on pit crews at the racetracks. I do not know much about cars, just how to put the gas and oil in when it needs it. Other than that, I'm like everyone else; I need a mechanic. The only difference is, I can walk up to a car and put my hand on it and see what is wrong with it. Most of the time, I do not know what it is I am seeing, so I must describe it. Most mechanics know what I see by the description I give them, since they know the inner workings of the motor.

The Dead

I am also what is known as a Clairvoyant (seeing the dead), and I am Clairaudient (hearing the dead). The only way to explain what I mean by talking to the dead is to give you an example. One is going to cemeteries. When you go to a cemetery, you see headstones, but not the spirits of the people buried there. When I visit cemeteries, I see the spirits of the people that are laid to rest there. I see them as they were in life, moving and trying to talk to the living that visit them. Seeing them standing with family members, beside their own gravesides is a moving experience. The family feels the loss of the person that has passed away, not knowing that he or she is there with them at that moment, if only they could reach out and touch them. I see the pain of the living that are grieving for their loved ones, because he cannot ease the sense of loss of the living or tell them that he is there.

People feel that death is the end of our existence, that loved ones are gone from us forever, not understanding that death is just a transition from one dimension to another. Just the fact that someone dies does not mean he or she is gone from us.

Cemeteries are an example of places where I see this, where I witness the pain of all those involved. Both the living and dead.

These are some of the hardest times for me. The loved ones who have passed on want me to give the family messages, to tell them they love them and not to worry because the pain is over, and they have gone to a better place. I just cannot walk up to someone who doesn't know me and tell him something like this no matter how much I would like to. Even though I believe that in some way it might ease the pain of their loss, I must stand back and watch their mourning, wishing things could be different.

One of the abilities I am requested to use often is about loved ones that have passed away. People ask to hear from them to see if they are at peace. It is not like you, and I would sit down and talk to each other about what goes on in our daily lives. I am a go between for two worlds. The spirits can hear you as well as me, but you cannot hear them. This is where you are crossing over into another dimension, another plane that exists alongside the one we live in. That's where I come in. I can see in both dimensions I pass along messages to you that are given to me by the spirit. I always try to ask the spirit to tell me something that only he would know. Then I relate this to the person asking for information. Sometimes that is between the two of them. This way they know that what I am telling them is true, and really comes from their loved ones.

I use this ability for another reason as well. When I am asked to come into someone's home to find out what or who is there, I must use this ability. Going into a house to rid it of a spirit, or ghost, as some people call them, is not an easy task. Sometimes they do not want to leave for one reason or another. Most of the time, I find that it was their home in life, and they do not want to leave it now even in death. Sometimes I find it is a family member of the people occupying the home now. They feel close to the family and want to stay with them even in death.

I gather information from the spirits, such as who they are and why they are still here. This is when I find out they are most likely family members that have passed on. Living members of the family, when asked if they know the spirit, most of the time are shocked. Most people would rather believe they are losing their minds than believe they are sharing their home with a spirit. When I am asked questions by the living, or the spirit, I try to find out from the other one the answer. Sometimes it is not easy to make one understand that he is dead or make the living believe it is someone they know and loved that has passed on. I have found that most people are open-minded, but not all. Some will admit to being so if they are alone. In a gathering of family members, most will not admit to believing it spirits. They are afraid of being ridiculed by other family members or friends at the gathering. Most believe they should hear the spirit as I do. Trying to get the living family member to understand why he cannot hear them as I do is hard. They are trying to cross a dimension that cannot be crossed by most individuals. They want to hear them and speak to them as well, but most of the time, this cannot be accomplished. However, the thought of a loved one being so close and not being able to touch him or her can be painful.

The Walk

Walking over people's land is something I enjoy doing. I love the outdoors. I am asked to do this at times when the owner wants to build a house or dig a swimming pool. They have even asked me to help them find old graveyards that may have been on the land, when they know it has been documented, but the headstones were later removed. This is something I do not really like doing, but will if asked to, because I usually find them even when I am not asked. These I just do not mention. Once or twice, I have found more than one graveyard on someone's property. Most of the time, they date back as far as the early 1800's or earlier. I have found gravesites that I feel date back to the Indians. How I date them is by what is buried with them such as those arrows, and pottery. I have found that time does not hinder the spirit from making his presence known. They have no sense of time. Life to us that may span in years may seem like days to the spirits. When I pick up one this old, I just try to let him know there is no one left to give a message to, and that he needs to look on the other side for the people he is searching for. I will try to explain about the passage of time on this side, and that the only ones left here are grandchildren or maybe great grandchildren. That the children he left behind are gone to the other side. That he has no reason to stay here any longer. That now he can rest in peace.

I have walked people's land for water, some call this dowsing. I don't call it that, because I do not use anything to help me such as a stick or some other device used by most people. I can feel water under my feet when I walk over it. I can also hear it moving if it is an underground stream and moving. I can tell how deep it is by the distance and firmness of the ground between the water and my feet. If it is not a still pond, I can tell by the sounds I hear. It will sound as if I am walking beside a small stream. With non-moving water, I sometimes get a taste in my mouth of stale water. If it has a lot of sulfur in it, I smell the sulfur, or just get a bad taste of sulfur in my mouth.

I have also been asked to look for oil on someone's land. I do not usually find enough to make the owner rich. I have once or twice, but this is an unusual happening. I can tell when I find it by a feeling or taste. It feels thicker than water, but not like oil you put into your car. The taste in my mouth gets slimy, and I get a taste of mud. Mostly it is a small pocket or pool of oil far beneath the surface. It has happened that the oil is closer to the surface than usual and there is no need to drill deep. Most of the time it is just enough oil to be aggravating, to me as well as to them.

With gas, it is harder to explain, because natural gas has no smell or taste. Most of the time I will walk over it once, then have to go back to make sure that I'm right. I do this because I get a dizzy feeling when I walk over it. It's not the same as experiencing a dizzy spell because of high blood pressure; it's different because it's outside the body, as if you walked into a swarm of gnats. It's more like getting light-headed. The bigger the gas packet the more lightheaded I get. If it is just a small one, then I don't really feel it strongly and must be careful that I don't miss it as I walk over it.

I have been asked to walk land for gold a few times. This is something I really like to do. It's a wonderful feeling to inform someone that there is gold or precious jewelry on the land. It took me awhile to understand what I was feeling when I passed over gold. This took a lot of concentration on my part to grasp the feeling of it. Now I know it when I walk over it by the feel. Gold gives me a solid feeling and it has a cold feel to it. I really cannot tell how much is there, but I can tell if it is just a little or worth digging by the solidness of it. I do not pick up iron or other metals well, if at all. I do not think that I would know what it was if I walked over it.

One thing I find a lot of is graves. I find that in past years people were laid to rest on the land where they lived. Some descendants of these people want to find their ancestors' graves. This is something I have been asked about before, when people want to know about the land and just what is on it. It is quite common for people in this age to search the records of prior owners of land that is now in their possession.

Another is caves. In Kentucky, caves have been found to run underground in all directions. There are quite a few of them documented. There is one large one, well known in Hopkinsville, which is from one end of the city to the other. It is a well-known fact that underneath Christian County is a maze of underground caves of every size and shape. I have been asked about this when I walk people's land. If the land they own has many caves, I can tell by the feel of solidness under my feet. If the ground between me and the cave is enough distance for what they want to dig for, then I tell them what I find. I have found that in some places there is less than a few feet of distance between the surface and the cave. If I walk over ground that is not very deep, I get the feeling that the bottom is falling out from under my feet. If not, then the land has enough soil to dig there.

As I said before, I am never alone. Walking people's land is one of the times I really have company. There are people who go out into the country to be alone, to just enjoy the peace and quiet. For me, I pick up spirits more there than anywhere else. I pick up spirits from hundreds of years ago. I see people working the land with horses and mules, plowing the land as if they had never left. I see people whose land this was, and their spirits are still here, going about their daily lives as if time had stood still. I see children and animals running and playing, as they did in life. I can tell they are from years gone by because of their clothing. There are no cars or trucks, and there are cabins where now would be big fine homes. In one way, this is good. I have learned one thing from this: that money cannot buy you happiness. I see poor people living a life that no one in this day and time would live. I know that a lot of us have not realized what we have and how hard it was for the families of the past.

Readings

I have been doing psychic and tarot card readings for more than twenty-five years. People come to me from all parts of the United States. I read them over the phone as well as in person. I would prefer to do readings in person, but sometimes it is just not feasible.

When reading for a person, I usually invite him or her to my home. When I do readings at home, I ask him to sit across from me at my dining table. I find it is easier to read for people if they are seated comfortably and at ease. Most seem to think that they will be taken into a dark room with crystal balls and burning candles as seen on television. I know there are psychics that do use this type of atmosphere, but I do not care for this kind of theatrics. I invite my clients in and offer them coffee or something else to drink. I talk to them for a few minutes and tell them how I do readings.

I get my tarot cards out and ask them if they would like to use them. I do not need them, but some people are used to seeing them. I first ask them if they have questions if there is, I answer any question they have first, and then I tell them what I see.

When I say see, I mean that I see a picture in my mind. I receive pictures of people or places. I describe in detail as much as possible of what it is I see. Sometimes I can give names, but not always. I can see people in their lives now or in the past. I feel that if you can tell someone something about his past that you could not have known it is easier for them to believe what you tell them about the future this way. I may see them taking a trip, or a new baby coming into their lives.

One of the most frequently asked questions is about their love lives. If I see someone coming into your life, most of the time I can tell you what he or she will look like. I will not tell you I see someone if I do not. I do not just tell you what you want to hear. I always say "Don't ask me something if you don't want to hear the answer". I believe that if a person goes to a psychic there is something he wants to know. However, people coming for readings do not come to hear lies. They may be lonely and want someone in their lives as we all do. I hate to tell them I do not see anyone for them.

Another question I am asked is, "Will I be rich?" I answer this by what I see. If I see a large amount of money, I tell them; if not I tell them what amount range I do see. I know the difference by the way it feels. If it is a large amount, I will feel a lot of energy; if not then I know it is a small amount. I'm not out to tell someone that he is going to win the lottery and be rich; I do see people winning sometimes but not often and not large amounts of money.

The one thing I do not ever relate to people is death. I do not believe that it is my place to do this. I feel it is hard enough for people to get by day to day, without having to know they are going to die. This is something I know, but if given the choice do not want to know. The main reason is I do not feel that I should play God. It is his job, not mine.

Most people ask me about their children. I feel great when I can tell them I see good things coming for them. I have children, and I know I want the best for them as any parent would. I hate the part when they ask me about what their children are doing. By this I mean, often they want to know if they are on drugs or drinking too much. I do not like to tell them their children are headed for trouble. I try to break it to them in a way I feel I would want to hear it, coming from someone else. We want to feel good about our children and believe in the best. I am glad for my abilities when it comes to being able to let a parent know that something is wrong with her child that can be cured, and how to go about getting help.

I get the funniest looks when I tell people I can read animals as well as I do people. The first thing they ask is 'how?" I do not know how I do this. I just know that I can touch animals and know what is going on with them.

Dogs and cats have about a five -to- six- year memory span. I can pick up pictures of past owners, and how they treated their pets. I can tell if they feel lonesome, and if they miss mates or people from their past. I have come to understand that they do not really know what is going on around them when they change families, or why the people they love are gone. I do know that they understand death better than most people. They attach themselves to the person's soul as well as the person's body. In addition, when someone dies, they know the soul is gone.

They both, dogs and cats can pick up spirits better than we humans can. They can see people that have passed away quicker and more clearly than humans can. They do not have to see the spirit to know it is there. They notice it as the energy of the spirit moves around them. I have found that my dogs pick them up faster than I do, and I have had them to bring spirits to my attention because I have my mind on something else. I have had them start barking when no other humans were around. I knew that a spirit was close by, or I would see them around me. I would try to pass it off as their barking at something else altogether. Most of the time it works, but not every time. I have had people look around them feeling something but not knowing what. This is where undeveloped psychic ability comes into play. They pick up unseen energy around them but do not understand what they are noticing. I do not enlighten them. I do not know how they would take it, or if they would understand.

Horses have a longer memory than dogs and cats. I have found that they can remember ten or fifteen years into their past. I discovered this when a woman asked me to her home to do readings for some of her friends. As I started to leave, she said something about her horses. I told her I could look. She wanted to know how the horses were dealing with their new home, and if they missed the people, they had left. She had just purchased them and was trying to get a better understanding of what was going on.

I reached out my hand and touched a horse's nose. I could see an old man brushing him. When I described to her the man I saw, she said this was the last owner of the horse. She told me they had come to own the horse because of his death. I also picked up a woman about sixty; salt pepper hair was a stocky build. I could tell that the woman I saw had been a happy person. The new owner told me that this older woman would go to the store just for apples just for the horses. The new owner told me they were not eating right. I told her it was because the horses were missing the former owner, and that it would be a while before everything was straightened out. I also told her the horses would be OK, to just hang in there.

Houses

One of the abilities that I enjoy very much is the pleasure I get from going into someone else's home and sharing the past with them. I can go into a house and describe the former residents as if they were there today. It may be your ancestor or the ancestor of someone you know. It may be a home that has just come into your possession. Even so, I get to share with you, my findings. I find that knowing who lived in their home before them is something that many people are interested in. Most of the homes I go into for a reading are older homes that are rich in history. Not that newer home's do not have a tale to tell; but older ones have more history attached to them; sometimes 100's of years.

First, I walk around outside the house to see if I pick up the energy of a spirit there. You maybe occupying the inside of the home, but that does not mean that I cannot pick up something on the spirit from the outside. Sometimes the energy I pick up is coming from a structure that has been torn down in the recent past, most likely within the past fifty years. I try to pick up what part of the house gives off the most energy, and any bad energy that may be coming from the house. Then I take a look around the yard to see if the spirits left traces of themselves there, and what kind of people they were. I also try to see if there is anything else I need to know before going inside. This way I will know what to expect when I go through the door. Going into a house is something I take my time with; I stand at the front door and see what I can pick up there. If I find that there is no bad energy coming from it, I will then go inside.

The first thing I do is open the front door and just stand there. I glance around the first room I enter to see if anything or anyone is waiting for me, other than the current occupants whom I have spoken to beforehand. This way I can open my mind as to what is around me. This is also to let spirits notice my presence as well. I like them to know that I am not there to give them trouble, just to check them out. I tell the spirits my name and what I am there for as I walk from room to room. I have found that different rooms sometimes hold different spirits. They know I am there, and I do not want them to feel threatened by me in any way.

Some spirits are stronger than others and I have had them follow me through the house talking to me, asking me about family that has been gone many years. I find this unnerving even to me. I try to walk alone. This does not always work, because the residents want to see what is happening. I am put on the spot, because the spirits want to give them messages or they want to tell them they are all right. This is fine, but trying to make people understand that there is someone other than us in the room and for them not to be frightened is not easy. People say they want to know what is going on in their homes, but when you tell them they have unseen company, they get upset. Not so much today as they have in the past. It has become acceptable to admit the possibilities of unseen presences in their home.

I have found that the ones I like least are angry spirits from the past that are still there. I have at times refused to go into a house because of them. I have been slapped in the face by spirits, which have left handprints on my face for days. I have had my hair pulled to the point where I have had tears running down my face. Once I was thrown against the wall hard enough to leave a hole in the wall behind me. This is why I check the house outside before I go in. This happens very rarely, but when you are dealing with spirits anything can and does happen.

When in a house whose spirits do not welcome me, I find it hard to breathe and must leave. It can get to the point that it feels like someone, or something is sitting on my chest, then I must get out of there. This does not happen often, but it has happened, and it is not a good feeling. They have their ways of letting you know how they feel about your being in what they feel is still their home.

Many people love to buy antiques. They will go to an auction and buy furniture to bring it home to be admired and cherished. I have found that being in the same room with some pieces of furniture can make me feel sick to my stomach, and I will have to leave the room where they are. If a person has a mean-spirited soul in life, he will usually leave behind a mean and angry spirit when he dies. Pieces of furniture as well as houses can carry the personality of the person who owned them previously. When someone unknowingly buys this furniture, they bring this spirit of the of the previous owner into their homes as well.

Once I visited the Bell Witch Museum in Adams, Tennessee. It had been turned into an antique mall. I could only go into parts of the museum. I could not go through it all. In one room, I had to be helped physically because I became so sick, I was unable to stand. I have been back to the museum often since then and had no trouble. I found out the room contained some furniture of an old man who had died alone, without any family. He had not wanted anything to do with anyone in the last years of his life, and no one had cared for him during his illness because of the way he treated people. This is what I picked up from the furniture. That time I let myself be caught unaware. I do not let this happen often, not only because of the feeling of becoming ill, but also the feeling of helplessness.

At one time, I was asked to come to the museum to do a party. People sometimes get friends together (five or more) and I come and do psychic readings for everyone. This time it just happened to be the Bell Witch Museum. I did not mind doing this because it was something different. When I read for people, I tape it; I then give them the tape so they can listen to it later. That night after I had set up the table I use when I read away from home, I asked the first person I was to read for to come into the room. She sat down across from me, and I started her reading. Not five minutes into the reading, my recorder stopped. At first, I thought it was starting to go bad, but after checking it, I realized it was not the recorder. I could feel the air changing around me, starting to get cooler. I asked her if she would step out of the room while I tried to find out what was going on. I did not indicate that I thought it was anything other than the tape recorder.

I knew we were not alone in the room, but I did not want to upset her. Even though people come to a place like the Bell Witch Museum for a reading, they do not really expect anything out of the ordinary to happen. Such as being visited by the museum's namesake, who was known to have gone mad before her death. I did not know if this was whose presence, I felt in the room with me, because I could not see anyone. I just knew someone was there. Finally, I asked if it was the woman, they call the Bell Witch. I knew it was because I could feel the air get even cooler. I told her that I was not there to cause trouble; I was just doing the reading and then I would go. I told her that I did not want to disturb her, and I asked her to let me continue without any trouble.

I told the woman I had started the reading for to come back in. I did not say anything to her, but when the readings were over, I told the man who owned the museum what had happened. He said that it had happened to him when he had first opened up. I have been back to the museum to do readings since then and never experienced any trouble, but that is not to say I will not the next time I go. Spirits are so unpredictable.

Another home that I had the good fortune to be asked into was in Cadiz, Kentucky. It is known as the Broadbent House. It was built back in the late 1800's, and it has been maintained extremely well by the current family. The Broadbent's also have a store that sells some of the best country hams in the South. I was asked to do a party there by one of the family members. Having seen the house and hearing that it was haunted made it just too good a chance to pass up. After arriving, I learned that I had been the only psychic asked into the home by the present owners.

After I had read for everyone there, I was asked if I would like to look around the house. I said, "Yes that would be wonderful". The first thing I tell people is that I don't want to know anything about the house or about any past residents, family or otherwise. This way I know that what I pick up is not coming from something I have heard, but from the house itself.

It was a large room with high ceilings and tall Windows. The floors were hard wood and polished to a high gloss. Although the furniture was modern, it still fit well in its surroundings. Standing there I could feel the others had followed us. I usually do not like a lot of people with me when I go through a house, but this time I just could not say no.

Standing there in the middle of the room, I opened up my mind to let images come to me. At first, I thought I was not doing something right. All I was picking up were animals all around me, they seemed to be everywhere. I could see a big gray horse walking through the room, and smaller ones here and there. It reminded me of a barnyard. I stopped and tried it again. I still picked up the animals. I looked at Mrs. Broadbent and told her something was wrong. For some reason I was not picking up people, just the animals. This I could not understand. I did not know what to tell her and that I was sorry I had wasted her time. I started to gather up my things and leave when she stopped me.

She looked at her husband, then back at me and said that I was right, that the lower floor of the house had once been used as a stable. The owner had lived upstairs and had kept his animals' downstairs. Knowing that my mind was working on the right track was a big relief. Now that I understood what I was seeing, I could go on from there. Never in my experience had I heard of this. Now I was ready for anything, or so I thought.

We walked from room to room, and I told her about people and other things I was picking up. It was not until we reached a small room off the back of the house that I had any more trouble. As we passed through the small room, there was an old woman sitting in a rocking chair rocking back and forth at that moment in time. I broke one of the rules I try to live by. I do not like to speak to anyone until he or she speaks to me first. This isn't because I feel that I'm better than anyone; it's just because I have been caught talking to people that weren't there. This is what happened this time. After we passed through the room, Mrs. Broadbent asked who I had spoken to. I knew then that I had been caught again. I told her about the woman in the rocking chair. I tried to play it off as if I knew she had seen her as well. She said that others had seen the woman from time to time in the past. After I finished the tour, I told her that I had enjoyed that night, and hoped to be able to get the chance to come back. However, the next time I will keep quiet until I know if the person, I see is real or not.

There have been times that I have regretted going into a house. One of these was when a friend asked if I would look at her house. It was an older house in Hopkinsville, dating back to early 1990's.

It was a nice house, but the rooms were offset. By this, I mean they were placed differently than most homes. The dining room sat off to one side, closed in by glass through which one can see the terrace. The room was round at one end and square at the other. The dining room furniture was modern and looked a little out of place with the rest of the house.

The woman said she had the feeling that there was someone in the house but had been unable to see or find anyone. I told her I would look around and see what I could find. I was not expecting to find much, because I had been in numerous houses before and not picked up anything bad. I was wrong!

The first thing I picked up was an old woman standing, gazing out the window of the living room. She stood with her back to me, so I never did get to see her face. The dress she wore was pale pink, with small white flowers. It reached the floor, and only the toes of a pair of black kid boots could be seen peeking out from underneath. I could see the back of the white apron she wore, but not much else. Her hair was gray and pulled back severely from her face in a bun. I could hear mumbling coming from her direction, but I could not make out the words she was saying.

I told my friend what I was seeing and asked her if this is what she thought she had seen. She said she thought this must have been the spirit she had seen. She asked me to look upstairs. I thought it would be OK since I had been there before, and never experienced any problems.

Upstairs I picked up a man in the bedroom her two children shared. He was not very old. I could tell he had been in bad health while he was living. His age was hard to tell, but I felt that it was about late thirties. I could see him moving around the room as if he were putting clothes away. He made several trips from the bed to what looked like a large chest of drawers and back again. I could see darkness over his chest. I knew then he had died of an infection or disease of the lungs. Whether it was tuberculosis or cancer, I did not know.

We walked around the rest of the house, going from room to room. I didn't see anything that I thought she would be interested in, so I told her I had to go. She said there was one more room that she wanted me to look at. I told her that would be fine with me. The room turned out to be a small room off the upstairs bathroom. The door to the room was concealed by a hutch of some type. At first glance, it looked as if it was made into the wall. I hadn't been upstairs often and had never noticed this room.

She reached out to open it and took a step back. I could see inside what looked to be a small storage room. It did not have anything in it that I could see other than what I perceived as empty boxes stacked against the far wall. I took a step into the room and made one of the biggest mistakes of my life. It felt as if someone had hit me with a hammer in the middle of my forehead. The pain filled my entire head at once. The pain was so bad I could not see for a few seconds. My friend Tammy had to reach into the room and pull me back out. The pain stopped as I stepped back through the doorway coming out. I told her what had happened, and she said that her children would not even use that bathroom. They said that they heard strange scraping noises coming from inside the room and knew there was not anything in there that could make that kind of sound. I told her I wasn't going back there, because I couldn't take the pain that I had experienced while in there the first time. She told me that when she or her husband went in there, they would become sick also. She told me that when this happened, the sick feeling would last for hours. I told her the best thing she could do was close the door and never open it again.

As far as I know, she was the last person to stay in the house for any length of time. Not long after that, she told me she had asked a man named William Turner about the house. He is the County Historian for Christian County. He told her he knew of the house she was referring to, and that, yes, the man I had seen had died of tuberculosis. He had been approximately thirty-five years old when he died.

Pembroke, Kentucky, is another small town not far from where I live. It is not very big in size or population, but it has a peacefulness about it that many small towns would want.

Passing through, you will see homes built mostly in the late 1800's, still as beautiful today as they were a hundred years ago. I was lucky enough to be asked to go through one of these homes a large two -story home, which sits back off one of the main streets. It belongs to Ray and Doris Ethridge. It is a family home, which had passed from generation to generation up to the current resident.

Walking through, I found many of the family that had passed away long before I was born. The Ethridge's had also lost a child in past years. A daughter they loved very much died in an automobile accident. I searched as I walked through the home for this spirit. I was able to tell Doris that her child's spirit was still with her even in death. The house held good memories from the past. Not only did I find her child, but I also found a family who cared about the house greatly. I discovered the spirit of what we believe to be her mother and another thought to be her aunt. Both had passed away many years before.

It was nice to be able to tell her that she could rest easy at night. I hope I put their fears to rest not only about their daughter but other family members. It was a big change for most of the houses I am asked to look at.

Not only is it in other people's homes that I encounter spirits. In just about every home, I have lived in, I have encountered spirits. I seem to attract them no matter where I am. Since I returned from Germany in 1991, I have not lived in a house without at least one.

The one I have to say is the most memorable is the one we moved into when we returned from Germany. It was a large three-story house on South Main Street, here in Hopkinsville, right down the street from the one I told you about that I had encountered an angry spirit in the bathroom. It was built in the late 1800's and could tell a lot of stories to anyone who is willing to listen.

At that time, I had just returned from Germany with three teenagers and needed a lot of room. It had fifteen rooms not including the attic. My sister Polly moved in with us, which was something she did quite often when we were in the States. We didn't get lucky enough to have just one spirit, we had four. My daughter was the first one of us to witness the presence of a spirit. She told of seeing a man dressed in a blue cover-up standing in the dining room. She was sixteen at the time, and this scared her to the point she was ready to go back to Germany. Even though having a psychic for a mother has prepared the children for just about anything they might experience, this left her almost in a state of shock. At first, she thought he was just some man who had walked in off the street. She told me afterwards that she had never heard the door open or close. She said that she was about to ask him his name when he disappeared in front of her eyes. She knew then he was a spirit. She came to me and told me what she had just seen. I had not seen him yet, but I had felt his presence in the house. I hoped that none of the others would see him until I got the chance to check this out first, but that was not to be the case.

The first spirit I encountered was a man walking up the stairs. All I could see from downstairs where I stood was his back. He was about thirty years of age, and quite well built. I could tell from his dress that he was from the 50's era. He wore tight-fitting blue jeans and a white T-shirt with short sleeves that had been rolled up. What clued me in most was his haircut. It was cut in a ducktail, a popular style from the '50s. Later I learned that he had been shot and killed by a jealous husband at the top of the stairs. What this spirit continued to do was repeat what he had done right before the moment of death.

My sister Polly was the first one to see a woman on the second-floor landing. We had heard a woman humming on more than one occasion but were never able to find her. Coming out of her bedroom on her way to work, Polly encountered her. Polly said the woman was dressed in a long dress to her ankles, with an apron on. She also wore on her head what in those days was known as a mobcap. We had empty boxes stacked everywhere that had not been taken out yet. This was where the woman was, standing in the middle of those empty boxes. Polly said she could see through her as if she were fading in and out. My sister came running down those steps faster than I have ever seen her move. She was as pale as the spirit she had just seen. All she could do was move her mouth, nothing but air coming out. I knew what had happened, but when I told her, she just looked at me. She is psychic as well but had a really hard time believing anything she could not see until then.

One spirit that will unnerve even a tested psychic is the spirit of a baby. I wasn't the only one that heard it cry, all of us would at one time or another. We would then cover the house room to room looking for this baby. We knew that it wasn't alive, but we felt that if we could find it, we could do something to stop the crying, and help put its soul to rest. Sometimes my sister Polly would come to my room and wake me up in the middle of the night. She said it was driving her crazy hearing this baby crying. She's older than I am and has four grown children of her own and grandkids. Some nights after she would get me up, I would not be able to go back to sleep. We would sit in the kitchen drinking coffee until the crying stopped. Sometimes it wouldn't stop until the sun came up.

Remote Viewing

Some have heard of this ability, many have not. This I think is one of the hardest of my abilities for anyone to understand, even myself. This is not something you use every day of your life. Most people will never have the use for this ability. To explain this isn't easy. This is where your body is stationary, while your mind can travel outside the body, hundreds of miles away and describe some place you have never been before. This ability is used when I do readings on pictures of homes that I see in my mind. I can see places in their homes where a fire is about to occur, or where they will have trouble with water pipes. I see images in my mind that I feel they need to know about. I can see bare wires in the wall that, if not taken care of, could start a fire.

I can tell if there is a problem with parts of the house that need fixing, not only the outside, but the inside as well. I feel that this is an ability that comes in handy for one reason or another. I have been asked about this by people who just want to test me. When I start telling them about their house, knowing I've never been there, they really get spooked. It's something I like to do for people if I can stop them from losing their homes or someone they love in a preventable fire.

I'm not good at one thing. That is finding items people lose in their homes. People call me up and say, "I've lost this or that. Can you help me find it."? No, I can't. I don't know why this doesn't work, but then I have enough to do. I'm not asking for another ability. Not if I don't have to.

Childhood

When a child is unlike other children it can be hard to explain just what the difference is. They don't understand the meaning of the word psychic. They just know that what they see and hear is real to them. Children take what they see at face value. Not understanding that everything is not as it seems to be. What they experience day to day in their world is not necessarily what those surrounding them are experiencing. They just assume that everyone sees the same things they do.

I know how it feels to be different from other children. The difference is not on the outside where others I encounter can see it, but the difference is there. This doesn't make it any easier to live surrounded by people who are not psychic. Only the people in my home knew the extent of the difference. Others saw only what my family couldn't hide from the outside world. At such a young age, I did not understand how cruel words and actions of those around me could be. Not realizing that my family was only trying to protect me, I carried on the way any child would.

I grew up living on the outskirts of a midsize community, in what was known in our area as the countryside. My family at the time consisted of my mother, sister, and grandmother. We didn't have a lot of money, fancy cars, or a big house; but I was happy. My playmates and friends were the animals that lived on the farm, especially my dogs and cats. I had a lot of room to run and play in the field behind our house. At the time we did not have the luxury of running water inside our house. Water lines didn't reach that far out of town at that time. We drew our water from a well about 50 yards from our back door. This was in the late fifties and early sixties; in some areas we were behind the times. My mother and grandmother cooked on a wood stove. A black monstrous thing that took up a good deal of the room in our small kitchen. Today I can think back and remember the taste of the biscuits made in that old stove. Baths were taken in a big metal tub that you had to bring inside and fill with water you had to heat on the stove. I remember hurrying into pajamas because of the chilling air at night. I did not know then that other people lived different lives than we did.

I did not have other children around me at the young age of five or six to compare myself to. I grew up thinking that other children lived the same kind of life and saw all the same things I did. When you don't have anyone else to compare yourself to you don't think about it. You just learn to live the way you are. Taking for granted that this was a normal way of life for everyone.

Childhood

I grew up in Hopkinsville, Kentucky, a small town by some people's standards, even in today's world. It has thirty thousand plus people now. I do not know how many there were at that time: but as a child, it seemed as if the whole world lived there. It was the biggest place on earth to me. My mother would take me into town with her on occasions. We would shop for the food and other necessities we didn't raise in the garden at home. At the time the buildings seemed enormous to me. We would window shop for dresses, which my mother would then make at home on her sewing machine. She was a very talented woman and to me they were the most beautiful clothes in the world.

As I grew older, and started school, the difference between the other children and myself started to become apparent. I would know something before it happened and try to let those around me knows. As a small child I didn't understand that this knowledge would be received with anything other than acceptance, not realizing that people around me would be frightened by the knowledge. This soon became apparent at school. It started out with the teachers believing that I was making up stories just to get attention. When they found out this was not the case, from fear of the unknown, they would seat me as far away from the other children in the classroom as possible. No one ever discussed it or spoke of it. This was not something you discussed openly about to others. Nobody understood it, only that it wasn't a normal happening. At playtime I would sit on the steps and watch the other children playing on the playground. I was not asked to participate when they played games, because they thought there was something wrong with me, because of the sitting arrangements in class. They did not know what it was, just that I wasn't one of them.

Going home after school was the best part of my day. My mother worked as the nurse's aide and my grandmother stayed home and took care of the house. She seemed ancient even when I was a young child. She was Cherokee Indian with dark hair, tall and slim. Her high cheekbones told of her heritage, her eyes held love and kindness, but could change in a moment's notice. Even though she loved me, I would sometimes receive that icy stare when I misbehaved.

I would arrive home after school, and she would ask how my day went. When I would tell her about how the other children still wouldn't play with me, she would sit me down at the table in the kitchen and try to explain to me why this was happening. She would try to explain over and over again why others acted the way they did. She would try to make me understand that they just didn't understand how to deal with people like she and I. She would tell me that once people understood that I was just a child, they would treat me as they did the others. I didn't understand at the time that this would be something I would have to live with for the rest of my life. That for the rest of my life people would look at me as if I were different from them. She would then ask me to feed the chickens and the dogs just to take my mind off what was happening at school.

Like any other child, it didn't take long for me to forget about what had happened that day at school. At that point, in my life, I had friends at home to play with. Unknowingly to my mother we shared our house with one little boy and two little girls. I never knew their names; names were not important. What was; was that I had someone to play with that treated me as if I was one of them. It wasn't until after my grandmother set me down and told me that they were, as she put it, "not of this world." I didn't understand what she meant then, but at that age I didn't care. I just knew they were there when I got home from school and were not frightened of me and that I wasn't alone. We would play hide and go seek in the fields behind our house.

One little girl had light brown hair that hung down the middle of her back. The other had short brown hair. The little boys' hair was as black as a raven's wings. He was a few years younger than the rest of us, maybe about the age of three or four. I remember the little boys had hair longer than my own. I remember asking him why he didn't get it cut. He told me that he couldn't. I thought this odd because another little boy wore his shorts, not realizing that they were not of this world and that it was impossible for him to get it cut even if he had wanted to. The little girls were about the same age as I was, around five or six. They would wait for the time for me to feed the animals and do my chores, and then we would play together.

Few people realize that animals can see things such as spirits long before we do. They have a higher since of smell and have better eyesight than we as humans do. When it was time to feed the dogs, they would start barking and jumping up and down. They saw the other children and were reacting to the situation. At the time I didn't understand their actions concerning the other children. I would come to understand this later in life, when I would see the same responses from my own animals.

This was the start of understanding what was going on in my life, for my mother. She was scared to let me go anywhere near the dogs at first, because she thought they were trying to hurt me. I tried to tell her about the children, but she would tell me that I was just imagining them, that they were not real. She didn't see them, and I couldn't understand why. They would be standing beside us waiting for me. I would look from one to the other and back at my mother. Confused as to why she couldn't see them. You see my mother didn't experience the same sights and sounds as my grandmother and I did. This was a world she had a hard time coming to terms with.

She first thought that something was mentally wrong with me, that I wasn't normal, but in her way of thinking there had to be a medical reason why I wasn't like other children. She had grown up with my grandmother, but in my mother's, childhood, being psychic was not something you even thought about discussing. It was like a disease or disability you just had to live with, and you kept quiet about it. She knew while growing up that her mother had abilities that other children's mothers did not have. Such as knowing when something was going to happen before it did. My grandmother was quite well known around our house for walking to the telephone just as it would ring. Another ability my grandmother experienced was that she knew when guests were going to arrive before supper, and that she would need to fix extra food for the meal. These were just a few of the things that were kept hush, hush around our house. Only the crazy people you didn't associate with talked about it. The thought of her child growing up like this was unheard of. There was no way I was going to have this kind of life if she had anything to say about.

The hardest part my mother had to learn to deal with was me being so outspoken when other people were around. She sat on pins and needles the whole time anyone would visit. She was just starting to understand what was happening to me, that there was no getting around it no matter how she felt about it. Not knowing what I would say to someone when I would open my mouth and tried to join in the conversation, made her nervous. We would rarely have visitors, other than close friends of my mother's or grandmother's. They would be sitting around the table talking and I would just open my mouth and say whatever came to mind. My mother would go on talking just as if I had never spoken. Hoping that they would ignore me or had not heard what I had said. I would come out with anything from "you have a boyfriend" or "you took something you shouldn't have". You must understand that back in the late fifties and early sixties, this was a no-no. This was when children were seen and not heard. Having a child in adult company was very unusual to start with. We were sent out to play or told to sit quietly if we were going to stay in the room. I remember my mother giving my grandmother what I thought was a curious glance, but what I later learned was really a signal. My grandmother would then find something for me to do. Not that my mother didn't want me with her, it was just that she didn't know what was going to come out next. This to her was very embarrassing. Here was her child that she loved but didn't understand how to deal with and couldn't change.

After our company would leave, she would sit me down and tell me, "Donna you can't say things like that to other people. They don't understand how you know these things, and I can't explain to them about what you know." I would tell my mother "It was true, and she was lying." She would then tell me just because you know something doesn't mean you have to tell. It was hard for me to understand this when I was told that lying was wrong. The problem was that. As my mother she couldn't explain how I knew. She didn't know any better than I did, without letting them know of my abilities.

My grandmother would look at me and wink as if we shared a secret. She would know what was going on in my mind and tried to make it easier for me. My grandmother would take me off to myself and try to explain it to me in a way I would better understand. This did not always work, but she would still try her best. Often my mother would just throw up her hands in the air and say, "I can't handle this, do something!" She would get to the point she would ask my grandmother "Is there any way to stop this?" Knowing full well there wasn't. I know now that she would wake up every morning, praying that when I woke up I would be just like other children.

The times I enjoyed most were the summers when we would sit out on the front porch at night and listen to the crickets singing. Living outside of town made it nice and quiet, where every sound was amplified. A train track ran less than twenty feet in front of our house making such a noise at times that you couldn't hear anything. In the wintertime, I would lie in bed at night with my head and ears covered, on a warm thick feather bed listening to the train as it passed. It seemed that it was so close to the house that some nights it made the house sway back and forth from the vibrations. In the summertime, when we were outside, the conductor would blow his whistle as he passed our house. I don't know how many times my mother would drop what she had in her hands when that happened because it was so unexpected. You could hear her muttering to herself inside the house. I never understood what she was saying, but now I believe I know. It wasn't meant for little ears to hear.

Some nights I would play in the yard, where my mother and grandmother could keep a close eye on me. Sometimes when my mother had to work or she went to bed early, my grandmother would let me stay up late with her. We would watch the stars in the sky, and she would tell me stories about the man in the moon. I knew there was no real man in the moon, but my grandmother would point out what looked to be a face up there that looked down on you at night.

The hardest part of dealing with my abilities was in what lies across the train tracks. On the other side was the largest cemetery in Hopkinsville." Riverside Cemetery" It was well kept by men that worked everyday cleaning off the graves, mowing the grass and picking up trash. They never seemed to mind working in the cemetery in the daytime, but at night, it was another story, you never saw them there after 6:00 in the evening. There were times when people could be seen taking a short cut through the cemetery to a small road that led off the main highway. I knew at night that it would be different people I would see in the cemetery. At the time I didn't understand why, or that the people I did see were not alive, only that they walked the cemetery at night.

The first time I saw someone in the cemetery at night I ran and told my mother what I had seen. She walked to the door and looked out across the train tracks to the cemetery and explained that she did not see anyone, that I was mistaken. I could still see them so why couldn't she? I could see many people walking around, not just adults, but children as well. It didn't occur to me at the time that this was the same situation as with the children that lived in our house. At that time, I did not understand that being psychic meant that what you could experience was seeing the dead walk among the living. I didn't know then that what I was experiencing was something that my mother would never share with me.

One night when my mother was at work, I saw the spirits walking in the cemetery again. This time I ran to my grandmother and told her what I was seeing. I told her there were people walking about in the cemetery, and she had to come to look. She walked to the door and looked out across to the cemetery. She then told me she could see them, and that I was not to worry about it. That it was OK for them to be there. I couldn't understand why anyone would want to live there. I would ask about the houses lived in, and if they got cold at night when it snowed. She would tell me that they did not feel the cold as I did. Some nights you could see them clearly in the moonlight. I knew if my grandmother said it was "OK", it was. I did not question her knowledge of these things. It was then that she realized my psychic abilities were stronger than even she had first suspected. She was going to have to keep a closer eye on me now. She knew that if people could not accept my ability to know the unexplained, my being able to see the dead walk the earth would never be accepted. She had seen them many times in the past but had never said anything because of my mother. My grandmother knew my mother wouldn't have understood, and would have wanted to move away from the house we lived in. This was something she would have to figure out how to explain to my mother before I said anything to her. Needless to o say this experience would really upset her.

The problem came to a head one evening when I turned up missing from the front yard. Where most children will slip off to friend's houses, I would take off across the train tracks to the cemetery. I would see the children playing and being a child, I wanted someone to play with. They could not come over to my house, so I would venture over to the cemetery to play with them. I was too young for it to dawn on me, that there had to be a reason they couldn't leave the Cemetery. I had been told dozens of times never to go across the train tracks because I might be hit by an oncoming train. Like most children that age, I didn't listen. After a while, I would hear someone calling my name, but I ignored it because I was having too much fun playing. I had children to play with, and I was not ready to go home yet. I didn't think about the consequences at the time.

My mother happened to glance across the train tracks and saw me playing in the cemetery. She blew her top; she came running to the edge of the yard calling my name. I got the worse spanking I think I've ever had in my life that night. She yelled at me for crossing the train tracks, and then she yelled at me for playing on the headstones. My grandmother told her she was right, but that she had to see it from both points of view. That went over great! The yelling started again. This time my mother wanted to know what was going on. She asked me if I had ever done this before. When I answered truthfully that I had, she had a fit. It didn't help any that she didn't see anyone else there but me playing.

After a while she cooled down, and she sat me down and tried to explain to me why she was so upset, and the reason why she didn't want me over there. It's hard enough to have a child unlike other children, but to have a child that said she "saw and played with dead children" was too much. I remember her crying and saying, "Why her?" At the time I did not know what she meant. I know now that I have said the same thing a dozen times in my life: "Why me?" Now I have some understanding of how she felt. Because not only would I like an explanation of why I'm the way I am, but also if there is an end to the abilities that seem to keep developing over the years.

My grandmother finally realized that it couldn't be put off any longer. She would have to find some way to get my mother to realize that this was not something that she could change, or that I did it intentionally. One day she sat her down and told her that I was not the only one who could see them, that she had seen them for years, but that she had not said anything to her about it because she did not want to upset her any more than she clearly already was. My grandmother told her that this was something new that had popped up, and she did not know what else I could do, but that my mother would have to learn to deal with it. That if she was lucky, it would diminish as I grew older, but that there was also a chance that it could grow stronger as well. This was not something my mother wanted to hear. That there was a chance that I could be like this forever was not something you tell someone who does not have psychic abilities.

My mother's expression changed for moment as she asked me in a quiet voice, "Donna, do you really see children playing over in the cemetery?" At first, I did not know how to answer her. I thought she might get upset again. Then my grandmother told me it was OK, that I could answer her truthfully. I said, "Yes, I see them, and they wanted me to come and play with them." At first, she did not understand what I meant. Then as she realized what I was saying to her, her complexion became pale. She wanted to know how long this had been going on and why nobody had told her anything about it before. I made the mistake of trying to explain to her about the children that lived there with us. This was even harder for her to except and understand.

Finally, my mother came to realize that the situation might never change, that this was something she would have to learn to deal with. She was never going to have a normal child. That she had no control over the situation, and she couldn't wish it away. All she could do was accept it and hope that it didn't get any worse. My grandmother told her it could stop all together. At the time I didn't understand what the big deal was. My grandmother shared these experiences with me, but my mother didn't. Why this was, I don't know. It was something I just took for granted. That was the beginning of learning how to deal with and use some of my gifts. I had to learn that some things I've seen and experienced in my life were real and some things just weren't. I had to learn which was which. After that I would stand at the edge of my yard and watch the children play. I just played with the ones that lived there own our property. My mother watched me like a hawk after that, not letting me out of her sight.

I remember the day that my grandmother sat me down at the kitchen table and told me that the children in the cemetery were dead. That their bodies were in the ground in the cemetery, that their spirits or souls were what I am seeing. That they had gone to be with God. They did not have their families living with them as I did. They had to stay there, and the families would be with them again someday. I didn't know what dead meant, she told me that sometimes, things weren't as they seemed. That if you were good when you died you went to live with God. She never told me what would happen if you weren't.

She told me that I was different from other children my age, but it was a good difference. That God had given me a special gift and I was to use it for good. Not all people experienced what she and I did. Not too many people understood it, and that was why I could not tell anyone. They wouldn't understand that I was trying to be honest and truthful.

She told me if I saw something I did not understand, to come to her and she would help me to better understand it.

It never got any better, as I grew older; it never went away. We moved away from my grandmother's house a few years later, and things grew worse. Now my mother had to deal with this on her own, since there was not anyone there to help her. She tried, but it was not easy for her. I could hear her talking to herself many times.

I knew when someone was coming to visit before reaching our doorstep. I knew something was going to happen before it did. These were just little things we had to deal with on a day-to-day basis. When I say we, I mean my mother and me. She had to learn right along with me when it came to my psychic ability. What abilities I had, and which ones were stronger than the others were. I never saw a difference in people, I always saw them and the way they felt about something. I did not see a difference between black and white. When you dealt with people as I did, the color of a person's skin was something other people noticed.

As it turned out, when we moved away from my grandmothers, my best friends were black. We played together every day, and we were just about inseparable. Sometimes I slept over at their house, and it seemed like home to me. Their mother, Mrs. Nance, did not treat me any different then she treated her own children. To this day I still love her and feel as if she were my second mother. When we would get into something we shouldn't, she would punish me along with her own children. When her children received a reward for being good, I received mine along with them. She and her children are still friends of mine to this day.

One of the times at Mrs. Nance's house will always stick out in my mind clearly. To this day, it is still discussed when we get together. Mrs. Nance kept her flour and lard that she cooked in the basement where it would stay cool and dry. She would ask Shirley or Paulette to go down and get something. Both Shirley and Paulette would refuse to go downstairs where it was dark. After stating flat out that they would not go down there, they would both turn to me. I did not mind going down there, so I went. I always knew there was nothing that would hurt me down there. Just by the feel of my surroundings. In addition, when a light bulb would blow out, I still would venture down there with no trouble. They would stand atop the stairs and watch me as I disappeared into the dark basement. I knew where everything was located, so I did not have to search for anything. When I return, they would question me about what happened while I was down there. It was fun knowing I could go places others wouldn't think of going. Times like these made me appreciate my abilities.

There were times when I did not have anyone to play with, such as when Shirley and Paulette would be away from home visiting family or friends. There were times when my grandmother would come to visit us, and I would tell her about my playmates. She would ask if they were real or not real as I named them off. My mother told us one time that if anybody ever heard us talking like this, we would be put away. I did not know where away, but I knew that I did not want to go there. I guess this is not the average conversation of a normal family. Then, there was nothing normal about my family. When the average family sits down at night to eat, they talk about family, what happened in their day and about people they know. With my family, it wasn't unusual to talk about spirits, ghosts or what was real and not real.

I remember one time I slipped up and said something when I wasn't thinking. At times when no one else was around, I played with a little girl. Her name was Jennie. I knew at some point in time she had lived next door to us. Where there now lived an older woman in her late sixties with no children

I told the woman what my friend looked like, and that my friend told me she had lived in her house when she was a little girl. The woman said that I must have been mistaken, that she and her husband had built the house and she had lived there ever since. Before I could say a word, my mother took me by the arm and led me out of the room. After she had got me far enough away so that Mrs. Jones could not hear us, she told me that the little girl was probably her daughter, and that I could not tell her that I played with Jennie, because she would not understand. She also told me that most people do not understand that loved ones will stay with you ever after death. She was not ready to leave her mother, so she stayed to be close to her mother. I would see her with her mother as her mother moved around outside the house in the yard.

About a year later we moved again. This time it was to the East side of town. The house we moved into was bigger and had a nice fenced in the yard. There was a big house on the corner of our street. The house had not been occupied in ten years or more by anyone. The white paint that had been used on the house had turned gray and started to peel. Most of the windows had been broken out on the bottom floor, which gave it the appearance of having eyes. I remember hearing my mother asking others on the street who owned it and why it had never been torn down. I do not remember hearing an explanation as to why it stood empty. I do remember hearing people saying it was an eye sore that it was no longer fit to live in.

It was empty to everyone in the neighborhood but me, I guess. I would tell my mother about the people I saw moving about in the house. She would say it was a homeless person sleeping in there because they had nowhere else to go. I told her about the children, and she would tell me not to tell anyone else about them. That the neighbors would not let them live there anymore. This was her way of getting me to keep quiet and it worked. I did not tell anyone because I did not want them to have to leave.

In school, I still did not have many friends. I was still thought of as "the weird kid". At home I had other children to play with, but not until they came home from the baby-sitters. I had most of the day to myself. I would see the children through the windows of the empty house and want to go over and play. My mother would tell me it was not safe, that I might get hurt over there. That I could fall through the floor or step upon something and get hurt. She went over to the empty house one day to look around. I think she thought that maybe she would see the people I was talking about. I think she realized that I was never going to stop seeing the people at the house. By going over there, she could prove to me that there really was not anyone there. She went as far as looking in the broken windows of the ground floor. She never ventured inside, as I can remember. I think she was half afraid that she really would see somebody.

I eventually ended up going over there. I found more than just the children in the house next door. I would come to learn there was a whole family living there. I would see a woman and a man upstairs and down, but I never saw the children anywhere other than on the first floor. I would bring my dolls with me to play with. I remember asking the little girl if I could play with her doll, she handed me a little doll, but it seemed to slip right through my hand. That was when I realized I could not touch anything that they held. Such as toys, books, or articles of clothing. The little boy always sat looking at a book; I do not remember him ever doing much of anything other than that. The woman and man never seemed to pay attention to us. Thinking back on it know I feel they may have been from another time period. At that age, I was too young to compare any type of clothing that any of them wore.

Sometimes at night, I would see a faint red light moving around in the house. Someone on our street would see them and call the police. The police would look around and then leave not finding anything or anyone. They never did find an explanation for the lights coming from the house next door. Never finding even the homeless people my mother spoke about. I never said anything about it being the woman and man with a lit candle I had seen held in their hands. They would walk around holding them in the daylight as well. On Sunday's when we did not go to in church, you could hear music coming from the house. It was not very loud; it sounded more like a humming noise until you reached the outside walls of the house.

My mother even mentioned hearing sounds coming from the house in those days. I had heard it once or twice but never told anyone. I never ventured over to the house on Sundays because there was always someone coming to our house to visit. Back then it wasn't unusual for people to just show up after church and spend the day and eat supper with the family. I could never get away without getting caught.

About six months later we moved two houses up the street. It was bigger than the house we were living in. My mother started keeping "old people" as she called it, and we needed more room. That was fine with me, because I could have someone to talk to other than the ones next door. I remember one of the people that stayed with us was named Mr. Crombee. He was an older man in his seventies. He was a sweet man, and we got along great. He would spend time with me in the backyard, and we would sit and watch TV together for hours. He never seemed to mind that I was different from other children. He did not shy away from me or ignore me. He always treated me like a normal child.

I was still little enough to sleep in the same room as my mother. We each had our own beds, but on different sides of the room. You could walk from our room into the kitchen where my mother spent most of her time cooking it seemed. My. Crombee's room was on the other side of our room next to the front hall. This way my mother could hear him if he needed something.

One night my mother told me she kept hearing a knocking sound coming from the head of my bed. She thought at first, I was just playing, tapping on the bed playing tricks on her. She would come and check on me. Finding me asleep she would go back into the kitchen. After this happened a couple of times that night, she came in and woke me up. She asked me if I had been knocking on the headboard of the bed. This time she heard a noise coming from Mr. Crombee's room. When she went in to check on him, he was lying on the floor in a puddle of blood. He had fallen and hit his head on something. She called an ambulance, and they took him to the hospital. I never saw him alive after that. He died about a month later of pneumonia. She has told me about this tale many times, saying if it had not been for the knocking on the headboard of my bed, she would never have heard him. She believed it was happening because he needed help, and I knew it even in my sleep.

The one person I remember very clearly at this time in my life was the woman who lived on the other side of us. Her name was Mrs. Moorefield. Her husband had been a taxidermist before he died. We could not afford a telephone and would go next door to use hers. I remember the first time I went into her house, there were animals sitting everywhere. We stepped just inside to the hallway and that was as far as I got. I could feel my chest starting to hurt as we moved into the other room.

I do not remember what happened after that. I just remember waking up outside on the front porch. My mother said I turned pale and just passed out. I can remember the feeling of not being able to breathe. At first my mother thought it was from seeing all those dead animals in the room, I experienced the same reaction the next time I went I told her I could not breathe. This time she got me out before I passed out. Now I realize that it was the pain and suffering coming from the dead animals in the house. I have had it happen when I entered exhibits at zoos and other places that they show these animals. I can remember feeling the same way I did at Mrs. Moorefield's house. I could stand outside her house without any trouble, but I never went back inside.

We lived in that same house when my family experienced another tragedy. My cousin was murdered. We were both nine years old at the time of her death. I had never met her because she had been put up for adoption when she was just a baby. I had never heard mention the name Diane in relation to a cousin. It was also my first time visiting a funeral home. I had never seen anyone in a casket before. I had seen them dead and alive, but never had to go through this part of it. My sister took me to the funeral home to pay her respects. My sister Polly took me by the hand, and we walked up to the casket. I remember looking at a little girl laying there not moving or saying a word. She looked as if she were sleeping. I thought it strange because I could see her standing at the head of the casket, looking at me. I had never seen a spirit and a body together. I didn't understand then what it meant. I also remember my sister saying that she looked just like me, and that she wanted to leave. I could see the little girl still standing looking at me as we left. Outside I told my sister what I had seen and asked what happened to her. She never said much about it just that Dianne had passed away. This was not to be the only time this would happen to me. I do not go to funerals now because I experienced the same thing today. No one spoke of it after that day, but it was an experience that I will never forget. I have been to funeral homes since then and seen the spirits of those who passed away. It is not something that I discuss with anyone outside my family for fear of upsetting everyone.

A few years later, we moved again, this time to Carters Addition. I was about 12 at this time. We moved so we could be closer to my mother's work. It was not as nice as the one we had just moved out of, but it did not have as many neighbors and had a bigger yard. I did not mind this too much; it reminded me of living at my grandmother's place.

Childhood

One day I heard someone talking in the kitchen, thinking it was my mother I went in to sit with her while she fixed lunch. Walking through the door, I could see people in the room I did not recognize. There was a man and a woman and a little boy in the kitchen. I asked them who they were and received no answer. I asked them again and still they did not notice me. For me this was something that I was not used to. Dead or alive they would usually speak to me.

I went to my mother's room to get her and told her about the people in the kitchen. When she asked who they were I told there that I didn't know. I had never seen them before. She followed me back into the kitchen and they were gone. I knew they had been there moments ago, but now disappeared. She looked out the kitchen window, thinking that maybe they had stepped out the back door.

She left the room, and they were back, I could see them just as I had when I first seen them. I called my mother, "Mom, they're here again." This time when she came into the room, I could still see them. My mother told me she did not see anyone in there, I said I could see them. She asked me what they looked like. I told about the woman, standing next to the back kitchen wall doing something with her hands. I could not tell what she was doing, but it looked like she was cooking something on a stove that might have been there once upon a time.

The man seemed to be sitting down on a chair I couldn't see. I told my mother this and she asked me to point out where he was sitting. I showed her, and she asked if there was anyone else in the room. I told her that was a little boy lying on the floor asleep on a pallet. I could see he was about three years old. He had blonde hair and looked to be a healthy chubby baby. I thought he was so cute. After that I could see the people in the kitchen all the time, but they never spoke to me. I tried and tried to talk to them, but I don't remember them ever saying a word to me the whole time we lived there.

There was one time in my childhood that I believed this gift was a blessing. We had moved again, but this time into an apartment. We had never lived in a place like this, where there were a lot of other children around us. We had lived in a single dwelling house until now. I was about thirteen at this time, and still learning to deal with my whole life.

My sister had moved also, and now lived on the other side of town from us. She had four children then, the baby was just over a year old, and named David Brent. He was a fat little thing with round cheeks and walking well. I did not love him any more than I did not love Polly's other children, but he was the baby that received the most attention. It was like playing with a baby doll but with a real baby.

One night my mother got a call from Polly saying she thought someone was trying to break into her house. I remember my mother getting everything together for the night and going over to her house. Just as we got there two police cars drove up. We did not have a car, so we had to hire a taxi to take us to Polly's house. When my mother saw the police cars, she really became upset. She thought we were too late, that the person had gotten into Polly's house before we had got there.

After they left, we went inside and watched television for a while. Sometime later, my mother said that it was time to get to bed. Polly put my mother and me in her room in the front of the house, while she slept on the couch. I don't know how long I had been asleep, but I woke up crying. I must have been screaming louder than I thought. I had awakened both my mother and Polly in the next room. Polly turned on the light as she came in, asking me what was wrong.

I had dreamed that I had walked out the back door of Polly's house and into the backyard. Over in the left part of the yard there was a man standing over a small box. I could not tell what kind of box it was, or what was in it from where I stood. I knew that I had never seen the man before. He was big built and very dark skinned. I couldn't tell if he was black or maybe Spanish. I just knew that he looked like someone who could not be the bearer of good news. He gave me a look that would send chills down your spine.

There was a big wooden fence around the yard, and the grass covered the ground like a thick green blanket. The sun was shining overhead more brightly that I had ever seen in real life. For some reason I didn't understand I knew the man couldn't hurt me, so I walked over to where he stood and looked down into the box.

The closer I came to the box, the more I could see what lay inside. As I reached the box, I could see a child lying there. At first, I thought he was sleeping, and then I realized he was dead. The box was a coffin. Not like any coffin I had ever seen, it looked as if it were covered in white felt was little blue flowers around the edges. In the box lay my sister's baby David. He was dressed in a sleeper and had a bottle in one hand. I am never seen him lie so still even in sleep. The dark-skinned man started laughing and reached for David. That was when I awoke.

I do not know what I said to them when I woke up, but a few minutes later, we heard Polly yell. She had grabbed David and ran into the bedroom where we were. She said to call the police that the man that had tried to get in before, was back. She said later that the man had been standing at the window of the children's bedroom trying to get inside.

When the police came, they told us he had escaped from Western State Mental Hospital and was dangerous. I believe that the dream I had was a way for warning me that the man was trying to get inside. I think that my dream saved the children from being hurt. I do believe that God gave me this gift to help other people, but in time of real need he lets me see how to help my family.

I knew that as I got older, the more I would experience. I would see horses, buggies, and other modes of transportation not used in recent years. Not only would I see children, but whole families walking the streets of my hometown. I could not go anywhere without seeing things that were not there. I would cry, because it was hard for me to know what was real, and what was not. I had to teach myself what to look for when seeing others. To notice the dresses or hair styles. To notice if others around me were speaking to them or ignoring them.

In school I got along fine until someone from one of my old schools moved into the district where we lived. Then it would start all over again. They would call me spooky or crazy. They would not let me play with them, or when they did, they would tell me not to let their parents know. I really had a hard time on the bus. There was no place to go to get away from them when they started picking on me. Most people think of psychics as being grown up, but they never think about the child. They know only what they see on television.

I know it seems in this chapter that we moved around a lot. I do not know if it was because my mother could not handle the people around us finding out about my abilities. It could have been for work like she said, but I will always believe that maybe in some way, she was trying to protect me. I do not know if she was really helping by doing this or not. I would become comfortable with those around me, who to trust and not. We would then move to another location. Now I do not let it bother me, but at that time, it was hard on all of us

Adulthood

My life changed, as I grew older, in more ways than I can explain. I married the man of my dreams at the age of nineteen. In the beginning Tony took my abilities as a joke, until they started affecting his life. Then it was an experience to be reckoned with. His life would come to be a life of strange happenings and unexplained events. I knew at times he wished that he had never laid eyes on me. It wasn't any more than I expected, why it should be any different than the rest of those who became acquainted with me throughout my life.

While we were dating, I would make statements such as, "I think you need to call your mother". He would ask me why, and all I could do was tell him that I just thought it was a good idea. The first few times I think he did just to humor me. After he would get off the phone, he would give me this strange look, but not say anything. When I suggested that it might be a good idea to check the car out, he would ask why, and before I could say a word, he would hold up his hand and say, "Never mind, and walk off. There were a few times that he ignored me, and the car would break down. We would be stuck and have to walk to the nearest phone. I knew from experience never to say I told you so. I knew it was bad enough learning to deal with living with a psychic, I think that would've been one step too far. One time when I suggested to him about checking the car out, he gives me that I know nothing is going to happen look. I could see him having a flat tire. He ignored me and about an hour after he had left. I got a call from him telling me to come get him. The car had a flat tire. I didn't say anything when I went to pick him up. But I thought to myself, sooner or later you'd realize that sometimes my abilities come in handy. But that's a lesson you'll have to learn on your own.

My abilities really didn't start causing a problem until I became pregnant with my first child. I have always been told that at this time my body and mind were more open than at any other time since childhood. I guess this is true, but I never knew another psychic to compare myself to. I just knew that at this time I seemed to go through a lot of changes not just physical but mental as well. This was really my first experience with living away from home, Not only was my body changing, but my mind seemed to pick up on differed vibrations and energies around me. My senses seemed to be sharper, and my mind would pick up thoughts of others more quickly. As far as my other abilities, they just seemed to tag along with the rest of them. They became more enhanced the farther along I became in my pregnancy. The one question that everybody asked me after they found out about the baby was, "Why didn't you know".

You see, I was five and a half months pregnant before I knew I was going to have a baby. I never missed a period the whole time that I was pregnant with either of my first two children. I've heard this is not unusual, that it happens more than we realize. Living with a psychic can be a tremendous strain on a person. I saw how it affected my mother as I was growing up. I had seen how most people reacted to me outside of my family as well.

At first it was little minor things like telling him to answer the phone before it rang, or cleaning the house so it would look nice when someone walked in the door an hour later. He blew it off as being what he called woman's intuition. I knew there was a difference, but trying to explain to him the difference was like talking to the wall. I'm not saying that he never listened, just not to anything that had to do with being psychic. I couldn't turn it on and off on a whim it just doesn't work like that.

The first time he got a good look at what my psychic ability was capable of, it stopped him in his tracks. It happened one night in December 1976. It had been snowing for two days and the wind blew so hard at times that it felt like it would cut to into. They had closed the military base because of the weather so Tony got to stay home for a couple of days. There wasn't much to do but watch television, and talk. We lived in a little two-room apartment; with a little hole in the wall, we called a bathroom. It wasn't much, but it was our first place together. I look back now and think about the good times, and how they were the best in my life. We didn't have a lot. We were just beginning and like all newlyweds it was wondrous.

The apartment was just outside the main part of town, we didn't have far to go for food or the necessities we needed. The only bad thing was my family lived on the other side of town, and there were two feet of snow on the ground at the time. We didn't have a car, because I wasn't working yet, and he was a PFC (private first-class), in the Army. He didn't make enough money at that time to buy a car, so we walked anywhere we had to go. We would go to the park beside our house and throw snowballs and build snowmen until we were so cold we had to come indoors. The park was beside our apartment house, close enough for us to visit easily on foot.

One night we had gone to bed early, because there wasn't anything else to do. I think we had discussed everything under the sun, and finally ran out of topics. We had watched television until both of us just gave up and went to bed. Our bedroom and living room area were together in one room. We cuddled up together in bed to get warm and went to sleep.

Something woke me up about midnight, I don't know if it was my imagination or not. I listened and didn't hear anything, so I turned round and went back to sleep. About two in the morning, I was awakened again. This time, I knew I had heard a voice. I knew this time it wasn't my imagination. I listened; all I could hear was the quiet of the night. I could hear my breath coming in a slow quiet rhythm. Then I heard my name being called from the far corner of the room. I knew the voice this time; it was distinctive, I knew it was my mother's voice. I waited a moment and listened again, just to make sure. I heard it a few seconds later more clearly than the first.

I reached over and shook Tony. I told him to wake up, that something was wrong with my mother. He said we would go in the morning, that would be soon enough. I told him I had to go now, that it wouldn't wait. He sat up in bed and looked at me. "You really want to go to your mother's house this late?" I said, "Yes, I have to go, and if you don't want to go with me it's, you can stay here.

He grumbled but got out of bed. I could hear him saying that tomorrow he was getting himself a new wife, one that would let him sleep. I told him "Tomorrow, I'll help you look, but for now I have to go". It took a while for him to get awake enough to know what was going on around him. By this time, I was dressed, coat in hand, ready to go. I waited for him to get dressed, so we could leave. I guess he thought he needed to go with me, that I wasn't safe to let out alone. He wouldn't be the first to think that way. He would glance over at me every few minutes, to see if I was joking or not.

I remember walking out that door as if it were yesterday. The temperature had dropped below freezing, and it had started to snow again. I could feel the cold going right through my coat as if I hadn't bothered to put one on. . I could see a little cloud of the frosty air every time I took a breath. There was no one on the streets at that time of night making it seemed like a ghost town. If it had been in the daytime, we could have caught a ride with someone or made a telephone call. I knew the only way we would get there was to walk, and I wasn't looking forward to that at all. The only thing that would have gotten me out of my good warm bed is a "vision or a voice".

At the corner by our apartment house was the Greyhound Bus stationed. It was just a small building that closed at four O'clock for lack of business. You bought your ticket in the daytime and returned to the bus station when it was time to catch your bus. I always thought about the people who caught the bus at night. Standing waiting for the bus alone in the dark wasn't something I like to think about. I would have hated the thought of standing out there at night by myself. You could see the people from our house, standing outside in the cold stomping their feet and trying to keep warm.

As we reached the bus station, there sat a taxi waiting for the next bus to come in and pick up passengers trying to get out of the cold. It wasn't a big city so the taxis in town just rode around looking for people who wanted a taxi that late. We were going to cut across the parking lot to take a short cut, when the taxi driver spoke to me. My father had driven a taxi for ten years or more, so I knew just about all the drivers. The driver of this taxi had been a friend of the family for a long time. He asked where we were going, and I told him my mother's house. He said get in and he would give us a ride. I didn't need to be asked twice. As cold as if was and the need to get there, I think I would have taken a ride on a horse if it had been offered.

The ride across town seemed to take forever, but I knew it was slow going in such deep snow. He let us out and drove away. I could see lights on in the kitchen window and knew then there really was something wrong. My mother was in bed by ten or eleven every night of the week unless something was wrong. We walked to her door and knocked. After a few minutes I told Tony we had to get into the house I didn't care if he had to break a window. He said maybe she had just left her lights on. I knew better because she had drilled into my head to always tune them out as I left a room.

We tried all the doors and windows. In the front of the house there was a big window I looked in but couldn't see much because of the curtains. I told Tony that I knew she was in there, I could feel her presence, I told him she couldn't get to the door because she was hurt, I didn't know how I knew this, I just did. Tony was ready to take up on my suggestion and break out a window, but I stopped him. I told him I would go down to Polly's and wake her up and get the key. My sister lived just down the street from where my mother lived at this time, so I didn't have far to walk. Right then I didn't even consider the cold.

It took a while to get Polly up, but she finally made it to the door. I told her something was wrong with mother, and I couldn't get in to see what it was. She got her key, and we went back to mother's. We could hear a strange noise as we opened the door. We didn't realize at the time that he was my mother in pain. It sounded like a trapped animal in pain. We found her lying on the couch in the living room. Her moans grew louder the closer we came to the living room. She was in such pain she couldn't get up to get to the phone. We called the hospital and told them we needed an ambulance quick. They got her to the hospital in thirty minutes, but it seemed like it took a lifetime. The doctor told us her gallbladder had burst, and she would need emergency surgery. After the operation was over, he came out to talk to us. He said we had made it in just I time. If she hadn't gotten there when she did, she would have died.

The next morning Tony didn't speak to me for hours. He would look at me, and then look away. When he would leave the room, he would look back to see what I was doing, and if I had moved. Finally, I said." If there's something you want to know just ask." He was quiet for a moment then said," Why didn't you tell me?" I sat there a second then said. "I did, but you wouldn't listen to me" That was all that was ever said. That time!

I know everybody hears old wives' tale that they just brush off as nothing. No one ever stops to think that they had to come from somewhere. I learned at a young age that most of them had a meaning behind them, and not just to brush some of them off as nothing or meaningless. One of those concerned black cats coming to your door. This one had happened when I was a little girl and my grandmother said that it was a sign of a death. So, when one came to the door after I had been married about a year, I knew someone was going to die.

Tony and I had gone to see my mother one night and had just come back when there was a sound at the front door. It was about midnight, and both of us were tired and ready to go to bed. I told Tony if it was someone looking for me, I had gone to bed already. He went to the door to look out and didn't see anyone. The weather was chilly, and he didn't stand there long.

He came back and told me there was no one there. I said if they want us, they'll knock again. Just then we heard the sound the second time. I told him this time I would go see who it was. I opened the door and there was a huge black cat hanging by its claws on the screen door. I stopped and looked at it, thinking at first, I was seeing things. Then it hissed at me and I knew I wasn't. It made a sound that sent chills down my back, and for me that's something.

I called Tony into the living room to look. When he yelled at the cat, it jumped down and ran. I thought it was gone, until I shut the door. I could hear it on the screen again. I told Tony he would have to do something, because we couldn't sleep with the noise it was making. I tried not to sound like it was upsetting me, I knew from the past what it could mean. I waited a moment and heard it again. This time I chased it away.

I told Tony if it came back then it meant someone was going to die, and I didn't know who, but I just hoped this time it would stay away. When it came back this time, I opened the door, said I understood what it wanted and that I would be fine. I got the message. After I shut the door, I didn't hear it again. That was when I knew I was right. It was there to warn me someone was going to die.

Tony looked at me and told me I was nuts, that it was just a cat. How could it tell me someone was going to die? I told him what my grandmother had said. He didn't believe me then when I told him what was going to happen. The next day he went to work as always, not saying anything about what had happened. I thought about it all day. When he came home that night, first thing he said was "See, no one died". I thought I could have been mistaken. I didn't think so, but nothing had happened that day. Sometime that night I got the strangest feeling. I couldn't but my finger on it, but I knew the time had come. I didn't know if it was my family or his, but I did know that I was about to hear bad news. This feeling is one you'll never forget if you ever have it. It's a feeling of doom. There is no other way to describe it.

I didn't get the news that night, but the next day Tony called me from work. His mother called and said that his grandfather had died the night before. That she had waited until that day when he would be working to call him. She said that he needed to come, that he was to be a pallbearer. He told her would, but that it would be the next day before he could get there.

That night he told me he still didn't believe me, but that he didn't know what to say. I told him there were just some things that couldn't be explained. That we just had to take them at face value. I couldn't explain it to him. Some things I know in my heart, but don't know how to put into words. I have lived with it all my life, but it's still hard to explain to someone even if they do live with you. After that he didn't say a lot, but anytime something strange happened he would look at me. I had the feeling that sometimes he thought I was making it happen. That I could stop someone from dying or change the world.

It got worse as time went along. It all came to a head one night about five months later. We had moved into a trailer from the apartment. I was expecting my first child, and we needed the room. We hadn't been there longer than a month when everything fell apart. I mean things started happening that would catch us both unaware. For instance, the phone would ring, and no one would be there. We would hear knocking at the door and no one would be there. Tony was ready to pull his hair out and mine too. I tried to tell him I had nothing to do with it, but after what had happened in the past, he didn't want to hear it. His reasoning was someone was playing a trick on us, knocking on the door and then running.

Not long after that, while still living in the trailer, we had a visitor and not the kind that comes in the front door. We were sitting in the living room, while I sewed patches on his Army uniform. He sat across from me watching TV. I had the feeling we weren't alone. I glanced up not knowing what I would find. In the back of the trailer, we lived in was our bedroom. It was down a long hall, and the lights were out. I could see my grandfather standing in the door of my bedroom. It appears the light was coming in through the window, because lit was more like light glowing from the sun more than a ceiling light. I laid the uniform down and stood up. I didn't say anything to Tony, just started back for the bedroom. I didn't even look at Tony because I was afraid to take my eyes off my grandfather.

Tony watched me get up and by now he knew the look on my face. He knew that something was wrong, but not what. He still didn't really understand what a psychic was, and we hadn't been together long enough for him to get the full view of what could happen. I walked back to the bedroom never taking my eyes off my grandfather. I stopped at the bedroom door, not knowing if I should enter. I stood there waiting for something to happen. He didn't say anything at first. I asked him what he wanted and stood waiting for him to speak.

I could feel the air start to turn cool around me as he spoke. He said, "I want your first three children". I didn't say anything because I didn't understand what it was, he meant. I knew that I was going to have a baby, but not that I would have more later. I asked him why. He said," You know I love you, and wouldn't hurt them." I didn't know whether to cry or what to do. I asked him why again. He just said then same thing again" I want your first three children". I didn't understand him,

I thought he was going to take my baby, or something was going to happen to it. That was when I started to cry.

Tony was behind me standing there waiting for something to happen as well. He told me afterwards that he could hear me talking, but when I stopped, he could hear a whistling sound. I think that was when my grandfather was talking. After about five minutes the air turned warm again, and he disappeared. I really started crying then, not understanding what he had meant, and knowing in my heart that he would never hurt my children. I think that upset Tony more than the other events had. He took me by the arm and walked me into the living room, where he asked me what had just happened.

I told him what I had seen. He didn't understand it anymore as I did. He said that I must have been mistaken. There was no one there. That I had been the only person in the room but him. I told him, it was something that I was to see, not him. That he hadn't known my grandfather while he was alive. That I knew what I had seen. I sat running through the scene repeatedly in my mind, trying to find something that made sense. And not finding it.

That night neither of us slept much, I still didn't understand what he had meant. I still don't to this day. I do know that I have three children, one girl and two boys. So far nothing has happened to them, I haven't seen my grandfather since then, but I know that tomorrow I could again just as I did that night back so many years ago. I still miss him sometimes. He used to bring me something every time he came to our house to visit when I was a little girl. I don't have any bad memories of him, but then I was a little girl when he died.

Little things happened all the time, just things that drove everybody around me nuts. It's not only hard being psychic, but also having one in the family can be just as bad. One thing for sure it will keep everybody on their toes. Not knowing what will happen from one minute to the next.

While I was pregnant with my second child we stayed with my sister and her children. She had a big house on Virginia Street, here in Hopkinsville. Her children were small then, between ten and fourteen. We have lived on and off with each other since I can remember. This time was no different.

Tony and I had a bedroom all to us, and Christy, my little girl, slept with her little cousin. We would sit up some night's playing cards until the sun came up. One night after we had been playing just about all night, I said I was ready to go to bed. Everybody else was ready for bed too. We had just gotten into bed when I heard the bedroom door open. I couldn't see who was there because it was so dark in the room; there wasn't even a light shining in from the outside. I thought it was Polly coming into the room because something was wrong with the kids.

When didn't she say anything, I said, "Polly is that you?" When I didn't get an answer, I sat up in bed. I saw a shadow coming toward the bed. I could see that it wasn't a person, but I didn't know what it was. It hung about five feet in the air. Then as it got closer, I could see it was a coffin. It seemed to float in the air at the foot of my bed. I hadn't heard about anyone I knew dying, so I knew the death was still to come. I didn't stop to think about what I was doing; I just jumped out of bed and ran into the room where Christy was sleeping. When I found out that she was OK, I started waking up everybody in the house. Within thirty minutes, I had everybody in the kitchen, most were half asleep, but they were there and that was all that mattered to me. I stood looking at them. Each one in turn, seeing if I could pick up the feeling of death coming from one of them. When I didn't, I knew that it wasn't someone in the house, but I still didn't know who. I started calling everybody I knew on the phone. As I talked to them, I waited to see if I picked up death from any of them.

I called my mother at three- thirty in the morning. I let it ring until she finally answered. When she heard my voice she said, "What's wrong Donna"? She knew we well enough that to know if I was calling her at that time something had to be wrong.

I told her what had happened, and she said it wasn't her. After that I didn't know what to do. I sit there thinking. The only person I hadn't talked to was my dad. He didn't have a phone and there was no way to get to him but go to his house. I told Tony that I had to go to my dad's. He said he would drive me. I'm glad he did because there was about eight inches of snow on the ground. I was just about ready to have another child and didn't want to take any chances.

It was about one in the morning when we got there. In my mind I could hear his yelling at me for getting him up in the middle of the night. It wasn't something I was looking forward to. Since he and my mother had been divorced for years, he wasn't used to his life being turned upside down at a moment's notice. As we pulled up to his house, I could see cars all around it. I knew then that something had happened because at that time of night he would have been sleeping. My half-sister Sandy was at the door when we reached it. She told me my dad had had a heart attack. And that he had been rushed to the hospital, and they didn't think he would make it. Well, he fooled us all; he did it, but was never the same after that.

I have four sisters from my father's first marriage. They don't live around me and are not really at ease with me being psychic. They don't understand there is nothing I can do about it. They seem to think I should just be able to turn it off. I've tried to tell them that this isn't how it works. It's not like a light switch. Both one of them is psychic, and they don't have to live with it.

Sometimes I scare even myself, but this doesn't happen too often. One time I became frightened as I was driving down the road toward home. I had been to my mother's house, and she had told me that a friend of mine was in the hospital. Her name was Pinkie Lee. I guess that was her real name because I never heard anybody call her anything but that. She was a lot older than I was, about twenty years older. I thought she was great; she always had a smile when I was around her, and she never treated me any differently than she did others. She knew I was psychic, but never tried to take advantage of it. We spent a good deal of time together whenever we could.

On this day after leaving mothers. I went to the hospital to see Pinkie. I got just about there and thought better of it. I knew the family would be there and I didn't want anything strange to happen in front of them, so I went home. I knew that even in a coma Pinkie could hear me. Whether or not a person can hear has been debated for many years. Well, I know they can, because I have talked to them. It's not like talking to you or another person; it's a mind thing. Holding their hand, I can seem to pick up them, as if I were talking to them in the regular way. I know this is hard to believe, but it's something that just happens. This is one of those things I talked about in the first part of my book. I don't know how I do this, but I can.

It's hard to understand that the mind can work on its own, without the body doing anything. I have learned that it can be a entity of its own, that it doesn't need anything to work with it. The mind doesn't shut down just because the body doesn't work at the time. I can hold a person's hand while he is in a coma and hear them as if he were talking out loud. I know this is hard to understand, but it's true. I think it's because I can investigate the body and see the inside as well as the outside.

Well, I didn't have to go to the hospital that day to hear from Pinkie. S she came to me. As I was driving down the road, everything around me went black. I mean everything. It looked like someone had blackened all my windows in the car. I couldn't see the trees as I passed them or the road for that matter. The inside of the car was light, as if the interior light had come on.

Just as I was about to hit the brakes, the radio came on. I could hear music coming from it and knew it hadn't been turned on. I waited, because I knew this was something I had no control over and couldn't do anything until after it had passed. From over my shoulder, I heard Pinkie's voice. She told me that she was dead now, and that I had to tell the family that she hadn't died of natural causes, but that she had been poisoned. I was to tell my mother so she could tell the family; it was not for me to do. That they would understand her, and not get upset. She told me she would miss me and that she had loved me as if I were her own child. I could feel tears running down my cheeks. I knew I had lost one of the best friends I would ever have. I understood that I would see her again, and she really wasn't dead to me. The grief I felt was the same as everyone else's. I wouldn't be able to sit across from her and chat over coffee, or just talk about anything that came to mind. It was a hard loss for me.

I drove back to my mother's instead of going home. I had to give her the message that Pinkie had given me. When I walked in the door, she knew I knew that Pinkie was dead. She didn't ask how, but then I didn't have to explain these things to her. I didn't go to Pinkie's funeral, because I knew she would understand. To me the body they put in the ground is an empty shell; the soul has left it to go to a better place.

We fail to realize sometimes that all through life we learn, not just as children. I know that I have learned some hard lessons in this life that I will never forget. One of these is not to tell people about death. That it's God's job, not mine to do.

The first time I told someone outside my family, about the death of a loved one, is something I will have to live with the rest of my life. Tony and I were stationed In Germany at the time, in Kitezgen, a little town close to the Bavarian Alps. I loved living there; it seemed no one was ever in a hurry. This was fine with me because I wasn't asked to work on many cases. At that time, I could read my own tarot cards and find out about almost anything. I didn't do it often for others, but I did if I thought they really needed to know something. This was my first mistake. Tony hadn't told his friends about my abilities because they might not understand.

One night the subject of psychics came up. I don't know who started it, but it did. Tony was talking about it when this friend of his said he didn't believe it. Tony looked at me briefly before saying "Donna's a psychic". I don't know why he did it even to this day. We had talked about it a lot of times; both thinking it would be best if no one knew.

Then his friend asked if I would read for him. I told him no at first. That I didn't read for those outside my family. Well, he went on and on about it, so I told him I would. I got out my cards and dealt them out. I could see from the cards that his life had been hard and related this to him. He said yes and that I was right about what I was telling him. I told him I saw people getting together for a wedding and he would be asked to be best man. He liked that idea, and on it went. Then I came to the part that started the ball going downhill. I could see the death of a woman in his life. I could tell it was close family and a woman, but not who. I told him it would be in the next month and to get ready to go home. He laughed and said that no one in his family was sick that he knew of. I told him that whoever it was wouldn't suffer.

Three days later Tony came home from work and said his friend had gotten the message from home his mother had died. This was one of those times I felt bad for being right. I know I didn't kill her or have anything to do with her death, but I felt bad for him. It's not easy losing someone you love.

Two weeks later I heard a knock at the door. I was washing dishes and couldn't get to it, so Tony opened the door. I could hear him talking to someone but didn't know who. I went into the hallway to see who it was. It was the guy I had read for. He was just standing there, looking at me.

He looked at me with tears running down his face, and said, "You killed her, you killed my mother" I didn't know what to say I knew I hadn't done anything. He said, "If you hadn't read those cards she wouldn't have died." I tried to tell him that had nothing to do with it, that it was just her time to go, and nothing anyone could do to stop it. He didn't want to hear that. All he could think of was his mother was gone, and in his pain, he had to hit out at someone. I was that someone.

Tony made him leave and told him to think about what he had said. I knew that he would never believe that it wasn't my fault. In his mind I was the reason. This hit me so hard that. I told myself that I would never tell anyone about death again, and I still don't to this day. I feel that if God wanted you to know, it's his place to tell you not mine.

I saw the man a few times after that, but neither he nor I spoke. It wasn't long after that he was sent back to the states. I never heard from him again, but I still think of him often. He is the first person that pops into my mind when I'm asked about death.

Back then I was young enough to try just about anything someone asked me to. I don't mean jumping off a bridge or anything, but I did do some dumb things. One of those was a séance. Tony and I lived in a little town about ten miles outside of Kitizgen. I remember the apartment house well. It had six apartments, two on each floor. We lived on the top floor, and it was a nice place, with large rooms. I could open my windows and look out to some of the most beautiful lands anyone has ever seen; with fields of sugar beets as far as the eye could see. In Germany most of the people are farmers. One can see them working in the fields from daybreak until dark, growing food for the livestock.

We were all Americans living in the house. It was rented by the military for military family that hadn't come on the list for housing yet. It happened that most of our husbands were in some company and had gone out to the field of maneuvers. There were four families who had children, a lot of the time we just left the doors to the individual apartments unlocked and locked the outside door, so no one could get inside without buzzing the bell.

That night we had gotten together for a party, not a drinking party or anything like that, but just a bunch of wives sitting around talking about everything known to mankind. We had rented movies to watch and were drinking sodas and eating chips and dip.

It started out fine until someone started talking about the movie we were watching. I hadn't thought much about it until then. I love watching horror movies, I don't really like blood and gore, but I like that kind where something jumps out at you in the dark and makes you jump. The other women didn't know about my abilities, and I liked it that way. Somewhere along the line, the idea of having a séance came up. After talking about it we thought we would try it. All the children had been put to bed in my apartment, so we wouldn't have to wake them up.

We got together everything we thought we would need, candles and things like that. We set up the table in the middle of the living room floor. It was chilly out that night, close to the end of November. In Germany winter comes a lot earlier than it does here in the states. We checked on the kids and went back into the living room and sat down, discussing what to do because none of us had ever participated in a séance before.

We sat around the table and held hands. (Someone said this was that you do at a séance). We had lit a candle in the middle of the table and turned off the lights. We knew that no one could get downstairs, so we began. We all closed our eyes, and someone said to clean your minds. I should have known then that it was the wrong thing for me to do. When I do this (clear my mind), anything can get in. I mean anything. I'm like an open door just waiting for someone to walk through.

Nothing happened for about fifteen minutes. I was just about to stop when we heard a noise in the corner of the room. We couldn't see anything there, so we went ahead with what we were doing. I knew something was about to happen because I could feel the room turning cooler. I thought to myself, "If I stop now, nothing will happen." I tried to let go of the woman whose hand I was holding. But she just thought I was getting scared and wanted to stop. She was right, I was getting scared because I didn't know what could happen and I didn't feel like taking the chance.

Before I could get her to let go of my hand, the windows flew open. I could feel the cold air rushing in the room. I knew the windows were locked because I was scared one of the kids would fall out, so I kept them always locked. There was no way they could have come open without someone opening them. Everybody was still seated around the table, and I knew that none of them had opened the window. I knew then that we were in for something we were not going to like to see how to move around in the room without running over each other. Finally, I found the light switch and turned the lights on. They came on and then went right back out. They came back on again in a second and stayed on this time.

In the light they stopped screaming. I could hear someone crying but didn't know who. Everyone was pale as a ghost and scared nearly witless. We didn't know whether to move or stand just where we were. I told them I thought it was OK; that whatever had happened was over with. That I thought they should gather up the children and go home. That I needed to get some sleep as well. I knew that even after they were gone there would be no sleep for me that night.

I got my children back in bed and quiet. I went into the kitchen and fixed a pot of coffee. I sat down in the chair and didn't move until the sun came up. I thought it was the longest night I had ever spent in my life. I never have or never will do that again. If I am asked about it, I tell them quickly that it's out of the question. I will not do it!!!

I know some things on this Earth cannot be explained. I also know that there are things we shouldn't tamper with. It's easy to sit around and talk about something, but it's another way to do it. I know if anyone does attempt to do so, that things can get out of hand. It doesn't take much for it to happen. I have learned to leave well enough alone, and for me that's saying a lot. People watch the television all the time thinking that it's a bunch of nonsense. Is It? Do you know for sure what is and what isn't? The best thing I can tell you is don't do something like this unless you have someone there who knows what she is doing. I have learned my lesson well!

There are times when even I get upset about what is going on and not having control over it. I 'm not rich and may never be. I have learned there are things in life that money can't buy, like happiness. I didn't say that money couldn't make your like a little easier at times. I know being overseas, there were times I wished I was a millionaire. I could have gone home to see my family whether for pleasure or out of necessity. I felt this way in 1980 when my grandmother died. It hit me hard, but I lived in Germany at the time, and couldn't get to her funeral. I was married and that was where my husband was and where I needed to be. I knew how close we were then and how much I missed her. It started out just like any other night, with me giving the children a bath, and putting them to bed. Tony had worked hard that day and had gone to bed early. I was getting ready to go in a little while. I picked up toys and clothes the children had strewn everywhere. I seem to find this the best time as other mothers do to get things done. I knew it wouldn't do any good, but I did it anyway.

The bed never looked so good as it did that night, but for some unknown reason I had put off going to bed as long as I could. When I did get in bed, I was asleep as soon as my head hit the pillow. Like most mothers, any time you hear your child, even in sleep it will wake you up. This is what I thought had happened. I thought my son Dominic had awakened and was crying for me. I lay there a moment thinking that he was just making strange sounds in his sleep, and hoping he would go back to sleep if I waited.

I could hear the voice again and knew Dominic hadn't started to talk yet. I thought maybe Christy was up. I walked into their bedroom to check on them; both were sound asleep. I went back to bed, thinking that everything was all right. I got as far as the living room door when I heard my name being called. I stopped outside the door and waited. I couldn't see anything in the room that would make me think something was wrong. I knew that I hadn't had any bad feelings about anyone, but then this was different. I can't explain it.

We had a stereo that sat in the far corner of the room. We didn't use it much, because we didn't sit in the living room unless to watch a video or if we had company. I turned on the lights to get a better look around. I still didn't see anything in there. I knew the sound had come from this room, so I waited. I could hear a buzzing sound coming from where the stereo sat. I looked to see if someone had left it on but didn't see any lights on.

I turned back to go to my room when I heard it again. This time I knew the voice of my grandmother the second I heard it. I knew that she would have called if there hadn't been something wrong with her, a reason she couldn't get to the phone. I asked, "Granny is that you?" There was no answer. I waited a little longer and asked again. This time, I heard her say, "Come home, come home". I knew there would be only one reason for her to want me to come home, and that was if someone was dying.

I ran for the phone to call my mother. Germany is six hours ahead of us, so I thought she would be up. I couldn't reach her; she wasn't home. I knew then that something was wrong. My mother usually got up early, but never left home before eight o'clock. I knew I would have to wait until later to find out what was going on. Two hours later my mother called me, with the bad news. My grandmother had fallen and was in a coma. They didn't know if she would live or not.

That day and the next Tony and I tried to get the money for a plane ticket for me to go home. We tried the Red Cross and just about anyone we knew. We couldn't get money from The Red Cross because Tony's mother had to have surgery not long before that, and we still owed them money from that. I knew I wasn't going home; there was just no way to get the money. Tony called me and told me he had tried everywhere he could think of, but no luck.

I went into the living room where I had heard her voice and told her I couldn't get home; I told her that I loved her and would remember her always. I knew she could hear me; I didn't have to talk on the phone to her for her to know. I could feel the ease of her presence in the room. She had heard me and knew I had tried. Later my mother called and told me she was gone but had asked for me before she died. She told my mother to tell me she loved me and would see me again someday. After the call I checked the time of death, it was the same time I had felt her presence leave my house.

I didn't go back to sleep that night. Tony found me sitting in the living room when he got up for work the next morning. He could see I was upset and ask me what had happened. I told him and he held me and made me cry. After I finally got it all out, I sat down and told him the whole story, about the voice and the phone call. When he asked why I didn't wake him up. I told him I just needed to be alone.

Not much happened after that; for a while, life seemed to slow down. I got to the point where I was on edge, waiting for something to happen. By this time Tony and I were having problems. It wasn't much later that we divorced. He's married now to a normal woman, and happy.

I came back to Kentucky and stayed with my sister Polly. I married again sometime later. This marriage took me back to Germany for another six years. I had another son, his name is Richard W

When you first get to Germany you have to rent a place off post. You get on a waiting list for housing. We moved into a apartment on the second floor of a house. Our landlord lived downstairs. The husband was a Germany police officer, and the wife stayed home. When we moved in only the husband spoke

English. It was a nice place also' as big as some people's houses. I couldn't complain. I came to love them; their names were Mr. and Mrs. Price. After we were there a while, I got a tape to learn German, and begin to teach her English. Mr. Price used to shake his head when he heard English coming from his apartment, and German from mine. I even took German classes to help me understand the people better. I loved it there. I lived in the middle of town, and there weren't many Americans around me. I had to learn German or just stay home, and that's not me.

I had two of the best friends in the world, a German woman named "Gisela" and Maggie who was British. I spent most of my time with one or both. I don't think I could have made it without them. Being around Gisela made me understand that not going out around the German people was the worst thing anyone can do. Living in a new country and staying inside not getting to know the people is a mistake. After getting out and meeting them I found they are wonderful people.

When we moved into the apartment, I knew spirits were present. I could feel them, but never saw them, until clear as day. I didn't see him in the hall, but just as he passed the mirror, I could see his reflection.

He was an older man, short with salt and pepper hair. He looked to me to be about sixty. From where Maggie sat, she couldn't see the mirror, and I didn't tell her anything about it. Not that there was much to tell, all I could see of him was from the shoulders up. I didn't see him after he passed the mirror. I saw him just for a second.

Maggie had a look on her face that said, "I'm spooked". I thought she was going to run out of there and never come back. She didn't, she just sat there looking at me. I told her I hadn't seen anything, that it must have been my shadow, moving around between the other window and the hall. She knew better but didn't say so. Not long after that she had to go home to cook her husband supper.

I knew what I had seen and started looking around the house for him. I went from room to room waiting to see if I could pick him up. I didn't feel him there at all, and that was strange. I can usually pick (spirits) up if they are in the house. What I hadn't thought about at that time was that in the past the house had been just one home, not two apartments. That meant that he wasn't just in my apartment; he could move around that whole house.

The second time I saw him was in the bedroom, just standing there watching me. At first it spooked me because I hadn't known he was there until I turned around and saw him. I spoke to him and he nodded his head that he understood me.

This was all I needed. I told him I wasn't there to take his home; I just wanted to share it. That he was welcome anytime he wanted to be there. I knew there wasn't much I could do about it anyway, but this way he knew I was a friend.

I told my husband about it when he got home. He said he didn't believe it, and if he saw him, he would "throw him out!" That was the wrong thing to say; from that day on he never let my husband have a day's peace. I tried to stop him before he said it, but he spoke too quickly. I knew then that he was in for hell.

Later on, I knew I had been right. Things started happening when my husband was home. Strange unexplainable things, like my husband's shoes would be moved, or his clothes would be gone. I tried to tell him "You did it, you should just tell him you're sorry and let that be it". "No, I won't do that", he said. He didn't believe that stuff anyway, and he wasn't going to say he was sorry to something he didn't believe in.

I walked out of the room; he had done it this time. I couldn't wait to see what happened. In the hall I asked the spirit please not to hurt my children because of what he had said. I felt a warmth come into the room and knew that he had heard me and was saying yes. I thought about my husband and in my mind, I said, "Big boy, let's see you handle this one."

It wasn't long until it started. I mean until he started in on my husband. I thought my husband would go nuts. It didn't happen just occasionally; it happened all the time. He would go to take a shower and the water would go ice cold or hot. I could hear him yell and the next minute he would come out of the bathroom, his face like thunder. It was all I could do not to laugh. I know I sound mean, but I'm not. I just know what can happen when you upset a spirit. Telling them you will throw them out of their own house is not the best way to live with spirits.

This went on for a long time. Then one day my husband and I got into an argument. He left the house mad, and I was crying. I stood at the sink washing dishes and crying. I wasn't paying any mind to what was going on around me, until I smelled roses. Rose are not the flowers I would buy for myself, but I'll take them if someone gives them to smile and me. While there weren't really roses in the room, I could smell them plainly. Then a warmth came into the room, and I knew it was the spirit I had seen in the house.

Needless to say things went from bad to worse. After that my husband didn't have a minute's peace at all. He would ask for a beer, and I would take one straight out of the refrigerator and take it to him. He would open it and it would be so hot you couldn't drink it. Once it burned his lip it was so hot. He would ask me what I was doing "trying to kill him? "I told him I didn't have anything to do with it. He would just look at me. We found water standing in his Army boots; His beer would be hot or so bitter you couldn't drink it. Anything he could do to him the spirit did.

The children and I thought it was funny for a while, until he started blaming us. That was when I told him a thing or two. I told him it was his own fault that this was happening to him. That he could just lay off us if he was going to be that way about it. He asked me why I never had this kind of trouble from what he called" My spirit'? I told him because I wasn't so pig headed. That's why! I had my share of run ins with spirits, but nothing like he had. I wasn't going to change it either. I knew what they could do.

One morning I woke up so sick I thought I was going to die. I had the flu, and I mean badly. I had washed clothes and had to go down to the basement to retrieve them. That was three floors down. I didn't think I would make it. I got my clothesbasket and started for the door. I made it far as the bathroom and I was sick. I know I stayed there for ten minutes or more.

I walked out in the hall to get my basket and it was gone. I knew I had picked it up on the way out of the bedroom. I thought I'd go lie down and try it again later; I wasn't up to it at that moment. I went into my bedroom and stopped and stared. There on the bed were the towels and things I was going to the basement to get. I knew there wasn't anyone in the house but me, so there could have been only one way for them to get there. I said thank you and went to bed. I never told my husband about that because I didn't need for him to go through the roof.

There are times when it's better not to say anything. It can be hard on a person to live like this, not knowing what is going to happen from one day to the next. Not growing up around someone who is psychic, and knowing how they are can make for one surprise after another. I can't say I didn't tell him about myself before I married. He had been told that anything could happen. I will say that your life is never boring; there's no way it could be.

There was one time while my last husband and I were together that something happened, and I still don't really understand it. We were friends with a couple that were also stationed in Georgia at the time. Her name was Sandy.

I found out a lot about her as we because closer friends. One was she practiced witchcraft. I don't get into things like this, but if it's something you like to do who am I to say anything? One day she asked if I would like to go shopping and

I told her yes, but I couldn't stay long. I had to get back and cook supper.

We rode around downtown awhile until we ran up on this little shop in the old part of town. The houses had once been expensive homes, and you could tell they were maintained well. They had been handed down through the years to other family members, or so they looked to me.

We pulled up in front of one that had a sign about old furniture and collectibles. I didn't have the money to shop for much. She was driving and after we stopped, she got out of the car. I told her I would wait in the car for her. She asked me to go in and I said OK. Sandy had gotten out already and was waiting for me. I told her to go on in and I would be there in a minute.

Well, by the time I had got myself ready and out of the car she was already inside. I started up the walk onto the porch where I stopped as though I had walked into a wall. I couldn't see anything in front of me, but I couldn't seem to go any further onto the porch.

I thought I must have been mistaken and walked back toward the car. I stopped and turned around to look back. I could feel the wall right behind me. I still couldn't see anything; I just felt it there. I got back into the car and waited for Sandy to come out. As I waited for her, I thought about what had happened. I had never had it happen before, but I knew there had to be a reason.

I had turned to see if I could see Sandy coming out of the shop when the front window blew out. It sounded to me as if a bomb had gone off. I tried to get out of the car and couldn't get the door open. I tried Sandy's door and couldn't get it open either. I sat back and waited. I knew then there was some reason I wasn't supposed to go inside. I didn't know what it was but something or someone was going to make sure I didn't.

Sandy and the man who owned the house came running out of the door and looking around. I tried the car door and this time it opened. I got out and ran to them and asked if they were all right. The man who owned the shop asked me if I had seen who broke the window. I told him no that I had been in the car the whole time and hadn't seen anyone.

I walked over to the window and looked in. Not a thing was out of place. You couldn't tell that anything had happened. The only thing I saw unusual was an antique rocking chair rocking back and forth in the room. One other thing that found strange was the window had blown out not in, so what ever had happened had come from inside not out.

We left after the police got there and asked us some questions. I didn't say anything about what had happened to me or why I hadn't gone inside. I just thought it was better not to. After Sandy let me out at home, I fixed myself some coffee and sat down to think about what had happened to me that day. I didn't understand it then nor do I now, but I guess it's one of those things that can't be explained.

I still experience these kinds of things even today

The Missing and The Murdered

When most people hear the word psychic, they think of someone telling fortunes or the future. They see the psychics on television talking about what's going to happen to this person or that person. They hear of psychics in places looking for spirits and trying to find out how someone died. I do this as well, but the one thing most of us don't see is the psychic's looking for missing people or dead bodies. Yes, you see them on television talking to the families, but you don't see how they do it. You don't see the pain they go through, or the hell they have to put up with.

It's good that police departments are coming around in their ways of thinking. Many have come to realize that there are people who can see things they can't. Luckily, I have worked with police departments that have been open minded. I will tell you that I have run across departments that have looked me in the eye and said they don't believe in psychics. I can't say that I blame them altogether. There are people out there who say they are psychics, but are nothing more than glory seekers, wanting their pictures on television or in the papers. These are the ones that make it hard on the real psychics.

I have learned that the police don't call on a psychic, unless they are at a standstill, in a case. Police units are made up of very experienced officers who know how to do their jobs. The police have ways of finding criminals that have been proven to work throughout the years. Once in a while they will run into a wall and can get no further in an investigation. This is when they call in a psychic. This is where I come in.

While my husband and I were stationed in Germany, twice I was asked to help the police in that country. The first time was in 1986 in Butzbach, about fifty kilometers north on Frankfurt, Germany. There was a woman missing from her home, and she had been seen last outside of Butzbach. My landlord was one of police working the case. We talked about it, and I told him I would help if I could. He had never worked with a psychic before, and really didn't understand how we could be of any help. I didn't think I would ever hear from him about it again.

Two weeks into the case he asked me what I could do to help. I asked him if he could bring me a picture of the missing woman, and maybe something that had belonged to her. I didn't need to go anywhere. I could give him a reading from there items at home; He said fine he would try to get what I needed. He asked me if I needed to talk to the family, and I told him, "No I don't want them to know about me unless they have to." He really looked relieved. I don't think he wanted anyone to know that he had asked a psychic for help.

He brought me the picture the next day. I held the picture in my hand. I didn't feel any warmth coming from the person in the picture, so I knew that the person was dead. I opened my mind to her. I could see a bridge with a small house close by. I could tell that the house wasn't very big and felt that it might have been abandoned. I had no idea where the bridge was, but I could tell them what it was around. I described the bridge and the house and told them there was a factory near the bridge. I could see smoke coming out of the stacks. The factory was blue in color and there was something running from it into the river.

I could see her body under some kind of old car that looked as if it had been burned and left there. From what I could see, the body was still intact, but it wouldn't be for long if they didn't find it. I could also see what looked to me like legs sticking out from behind the car. He asks me if I saw rats. I didn't understand at first what he meant by that. He said if I saw a rat, it might be down by the river in Frankfurt. I didn't see any, and told him no.

Two days later he came and picked me up and drove me around Frankfurt. I didn't see anything that looked like what I had seen in my vision. I told him I didn't feel that she was in the city of Frankfurt, but someplace close by. A week later I got word that they had found her. Her body hadn't been in Frankfurt, but in a little town about four miles outside of Frankfurt. I was told that everything I had seen was there, including the burned-out car by the bridge. They had found the factory first. That blue color was the color they used for most of the factories around there. It was the location of the blue factory by the bridge that helped them locate her.

This was the first time I had worked with the police and wasn't sure what they would find. I knew that I was able to do things, like see the future and the past. I knew what I could do, but not how it would work with the police. They were different from working with my family. I knew I could hold something and tell you about it, but I didn't know how successful I could in working with the police. I had just read objects for family and friends. This was a make me break me case. That case turned me into what is called a Psychic investigator. I knew then that I could help others and that I could use this ability to help others; I wouldn't have to hide it any longer. I have worked with different police departments all over the world since then.

After that I was asked once more to help in an investigation in Germany. This case involving a missing child, not only was I sure of what I was doing, but I helped find the child alive and well. The little girl they were looking for had walked off from the playground in Butzbach. I knew her mother and was asked to help. This case helped me understand how better to help the police when I was asked.

This case turned into a field day. They had first thought that someone had taken her. The father was from Israel and had been deported for murder. Interlope had stepped in to take over the case the day before they found her. I was never told what else the father had done, not that I didn't know already, but I didn't tell them that. The man with Interlope was nice enough and said he had worked with a psychic in the past. I didn't ask him anything about it, but I did feel that he was open to the idea.

I didn't work on another case until I came back from Germany. I came back to Hopkinsville, Kentucky. where my family was. I like peace and quiet, but after the first case I worked on here at home that was over.

This case started out differently from the other ones I had worked on. I have been asked to help in the other ones. This time I was thrown into it, whether I wanted to help or not. The police didn't come to me and ask me for help; no, I couldn't have been that lucky. With this case all I did was go to bed one night and go to sleep. That was all it took. I know that doesn't sound right but let me tell you about it.

I found myself standing in a room I had never seen before. I could see a woman sitting in a chair, and a man standing over her. I could see his arms moving back and forth; I could see her feet and legs between his legs as he leaned toward her. I could see everything in the room as if I were really standing there. I could see vines hanging on the wall and I could see wine colored the couch and matching chair. Everything looked so real. I didn't know why I was there, or what was going to happen. I just stood there watching these two people I didn't know.

The man then stepped back from the woman, and I could see her clearly. That was when I knew I was in trouble. The woman had been murdered. I could see that he had cut her throat. Her head was tilted back, and I could see that she wasn't moving. She had on a cream-colored nightgown, and the front was covered with blood.

That was when the man turned around from where he had been standing and seemed to look right at me. I didn't know what to do. He was standing so close that I could see the pores in his skin. I couldn't help but look at him; he was less than a foot from me. He never made any move to hurt me. That was when I realized that he couldn't see me that I wasn't really there. This was what some call an out-of- body experience. He stood in front of me long enough for me to get a good look at him; then he moved out of my line of vision.

I stood there looking around the room; for some reason I didn't understand then I needed to know this room. I looked at the body of the woman for a minute, then the room. I needed to know the details of this room, I didn't know why, but I just did.

The next morning when I woke up, I told Polly that I had seen someone being murdered; She looked at me and turned pale. Polly moved in with my children and me after I came back from Germany. She was living with me at the time of the murder. I told her it wasn't as if I had seen it in my sleep. I told her I didn't know the woman that I had never seen her before. I knew that I had never been inside the house I had seen and didn't know where or who she was. I sat down as I always do and wrote everything down. I put it on a peg board where I can see it. I wrote down all the details I could remember about the house. I recorded what the man had looked like, not that I would ever forget his face.

I didn't think any more about it until three days later. I opened the newspaper and there on the front page was the woman I had seen being murdered. I couldn't believe it at first. I sat down and read what the paper had to say. It just told a little about her and what had happened.

The next thing I did was yell for Polly. I didn't stop to think about scaring her to death, just that she needed to see this too. She came running into the room wanting to know what was wrong. I handed her the paper and told her "That was the woman I saw being murdered". Now I could put a name to the woman and what was going on.

Polly asked me what I was going to do. I asked her what she meant. She said I needed to tell someone about it. I needed to let them know what I had seen. I told her I didn't know whom to call. I hadn't been back long enough to know any of the police on the force now. I didn't know what to do. I asked her if she knew of anyone to call, and she said she did.

That night at about twelve o'clock Paul Pullam came to the house. He had been a friend of Polly's for several years. He had just come off shift and could take the time to hear us out. He had met me years ago, but really didn't know me from Adam now. He didn't know about Polly's sister being a psychic; he just knew she had a sister.

We told him about it, and he just looked at me. He had never worked with a psychic before and didn't know what to believe. He asked me to start at the first and tell him everything I knew. After I finished, he said he had been the first police officer on the scene, and there was no way I could know what I did, that I really had to be a psychic, or I had done the killing. Well, this was something that had been on my mind. What if they think I did it? Would I go to jail or what?

He told us he would have to tell someone at the station about what I had told him, that someone would be getting in touch with me. He left about two-thirty and at three o'clock another police officer called me. He asked me if I could come down to the station, to talk with him. I said, "It's three in the morning, can't it wait until morning?" He replied, "Yes, if you need transpiration, I'll send someone to pick you up." I knew by the voice else." I didn't have to be told twice. I told him I would be there. The next day was Sunday and Polly and I walked into the police station at eight o'clock. I had her to go with me because I didn't know what was going to happen. I had never been there before and didn't know anyone.

I was shown into an office and asked to be seated. The police officer told us his name was Bob Lilis and that he was working the case. He said he needed me to tell him everything I had told Paul Pullam, and not to leave anything out. He was nice, but I could tell he was not playing any games. I could also tell that if he thought I was playing with him I could go to jail.

I told him everything that I had seen. He asked me how I had seen this; I knew the moment had arrived; it was now or never. I told him I was a psychic and I had seen this in a vision, while I was asleep. I didn't even try to explain to him about out-of -body or what it meant. I thought I would just tell him the basics.

He sat there looking at me, not saying a word; he never once said he didn't believe in psychics or that there was no such thing. I knew then that I would be honest with this man that I could talk to him without fear. He asked for everything again. This time I knew it was because I had told him I was psychic. He wanted to make sure he had it right.

He said he had to step out of the room and would be right back. Polly and I waited not knowing what was going to happen. I was to upset to think about anything but getting out of there. He came back in with another man, and they asked me to repeat what I had seen again, this time to the other man. I did. I ended up telling the same story to five different officers before it was over. Then when I thought I would get out of there, they asked me if I could put together a picture of the guy I had seen. I told them yes; I had seen him well enough to that. Polly waited while Bob Lilis and I put a picture together, in the end it looked enough like him that I was happy. I couldn't have gotten it any closer if I had been looking at him right then.

Adulthood

I thought it was over, but I was wrong. It was just starting. My life and my family turned into one nightmare after another. Not only did the other police officers laugh at me they told me, but that I was wrong, that no black man had done the murder. They knew who had done it and he was white. I didn't say anything, I knew it wouldn't have done any good.

What started, as little things soon became big things. I would be sitting with friends and family playing cards, and the next thing I knew I would be in the car with the killer looking over his shoulder. I could see everywhere he went, and every person he talked to. I could hear the radio playing and hear him singing with the music. I knew that I really wasn't in the car, but it made me uneasy. I didn't like to think about someone or something having the power to bring me to him.

I would be riding in the car, and the next thing I knew, I'd be with him. This got to the point that I couldn't do anything. My family took my car keys after the first time I blacked out and followed him. I remembered pulling into the parking lot of a cafe we all went to for coffee. The next thing I knew I was two miles from where I should have been. I don't remember how I got there, or what I did on the way. I knew then that I could be a danger to someone other than myself. It was time to stop. So, when Polly said, "Give me your car keys," I didn't complain; I just handed them over. This went on for quite a while. I didn't get much sleep, nor did the family.

One time I was sitting there, and I was in the car with him again. This time he was leaving the scene of the killing. I could see the car and see him as he drove down the street and threw the knife out of the window. I called them and told them where I had seen him dispose of the knife. I was told they went to look, but I don't know if they found it or not.

I was asked to do a reading on the woman who was murdered. I n the middle of the reading I picked up on the killer. That doesn't happen very often, but sometimes I get lucky. I did if for the police, I really don't know what they did with it, but was told that it came in handy. That was all that mattered to me.

They asked for my help several times before they found him. I was willing to help in any way I could. It got to the point that I was asked to come to court and tell the judge why there were so many police at my house all the time. I looked at the judge and told him he would have to ask them, that I couldn't tell him anything. I couldn't, the one thing that I believe in very strongly is not telling what I know. I believe that when someone asks for help, he doesn't want it to be known.

The one thing that did come out of it was a strong friendship between Bob Lilies and me. He is now my go between with other police departments. I tell them to call him and if he feels that I can be of help, he will let me know. I have worked with others in the department, but he is the one that I work best with. I have come to rely on his judgment about a lot of things. I feel that he knows the best way to handle other departments. He is a good man, and I have found him to be fair to others. I owe him a lot, and I don't know if I would be working with the police if it hadn't been for him. They have cases ongoing now and if I pick up anything on them, I go to him with it. I tell him to do what he wants with it. I don't want the publicity, and I am more than willing to stay in the background.

In another case I didn't know how they would take what I had to tell them. There had been another murder in a small town right outside of Hopkinsville. This time it was a policeman. His name was Danny Pollard. For me the case started one night about eleven o'clock. The only people at home were Dominic, my oldest son, and I. I was putting a puzzle together and he was watching television.

The phone rang in the kitchen, and he asked me to answer it. He said he didn't want to talk to anyone. I went to the kitchen and picked up the receiver. All I heard on the other end was dead silences. If you have ever had your phone disconnected, you will understand. There is nothing, not even a hiss on the other end. That's what I heard nothing. I knew I had paid the bill, but anything is possible. I waited for a second before hearing a voice say, "Donna, this is Danny, the answer you're looking for is in the cards." I didn't understand because I didn't know any Danny that would be calling me like this. I didn't say anything, and then he said, "Look in the cards". Next the dial tone came back on. I couldn't believe it.

Nothing like this had ever happened to me before. I had heard about the killing just like everyone else, but I had never met the man. I didn't know why he would be calling me. No one had called and asked me for help. And I didn't really want to stick my nose in it. But I felt that if Danny Pollard felt I could help, then I shouldn't just brush it off. He wanted me to do something, but I didn't know what.

I walked into the other room and got out my tarot cards. I knew Danny hadn't known about them, so there had to be a reason for him to tell to look in them. I dealt out the cards, and sure enough there it was. It was all there. That his wife hadn't done the killing but knew who had. I also discovered that she was covering for someone, but if confronted she would confess.

I called Detective. Lilies and told him I needed to see him, because something had come up, and I felt he needed to know about it. When he got there, I told him about the phone call. By now he had learned that with me anything is possible when it comes to the dead. He sat there and didn't say anything for a few minutes, then asked if I was sure of what I was telling him. I told him I was as sure as I could be. That nothing like this had ever happened to me before, I didn't know how much of it to believe myself. I just knew that it had been Danny Pollard on the other end of the phone. I told him to take what I had written down and do what he saw fit to do. I didn't have anything to do with it after I gave it to him.

He left and I didn't hear anything about it for a few days. Then one afternoon Polly and I were talking, and I just blanked out. One minute I was having coffee, the next I was standing with a bunch of people I didn't know. I looked around and began to recognize a few people there. I was at Danny Pollard's funeral. I could see Detective. Lilies and a few other officers I had come to know. The one thing I did know was the man I was standing behind was the killer. I couldn't see his face, but knew I was right. There was only one reason I could think of why I was there, and that was because the killer was there. I was there to see him, and to let the police know that he was there.

When they did find the killer, it turned out to be her brother. He got life in prison; she was sent to prison but ended up getting a pardon from the governor.

There are times when being a psychic can drive you crazy. These are the times when you can't get anyone to listen to you. This happened to me a few years back when a little boy wandered off from his family. I heard it on the news and spent the whole day trying to find someone in charge of the search for him. I finally did find someone and told him "I can see the helicopters flying over where the little boy is lying." If you tell them to look down to the right, they will find him. I told them what he was wearing, and I knew that had not been reported on television. This way they would know I was right. I talked until I was blue in the face trying to get the man to listen, but he never did. A week later they found the little boy, right where I told them he would be. The next day I called the man I had talked to and gave him a piece of my mind. I know I wasn't very nice, but then I'm a mother too. If it had been my child out there lost, and someone called in. I don't care who. I would have wanted the authorities to look. The bad part was I had told him who to call to check me out. I could give him the names of people I had worked with. He still didn't want to believe in psychics. I know you can't make a person believe in something if he doesn't want to, but at least when someone calls you and can give you names, give her the chance to prove to you they are real. It could save someone's life.

One case I was asked for information about was the Taco Bell murders in Clarksville, Tennessee. I had seen the news story and knew it could have been here. Clarksville is just eleven miles down the road from here, just over the state line. This is one case that will stick in the minds of everyone around close to the killings. Clarksville is bigger than Hopkinsville, and a lot of people from here go there to shop. Many here knew the victims in the killing.

When asked, I told them I saw a white guy and a black guy doing the killing. I could see them as clearly as if I had been there. I also told them what kind of gun was used in the killing. I could see the bodies in the back room, and how they were sitting. I knew the make, model, and color of the car they were driving. I gave Detective. Lilis a description of the men and told him that I would help if needed. Since the killings happened in another state, they never came to me for help.

About a year after they caught the African American, they caught a white guy and brought him to trial. It was then that Detective Lilis told me he remembered my telling him about the white guy in the killings. It was nice to know that someone had believed in me, when it was hard to get anyone to believe in my psychic abilities.

I have found that involvement in one case may end up on another. This is what happened to me in one case I worked on in Tennessee. If I feel that I can be of help in any case I will try. I had gone to Shelbyville, Tennessee, looking for a man who had walked off from his home. They had come to a standstill in the case and didn't have anything to lose.

Again, this was a case I picked up from the television, while watching the news in Nashville. I knew the man was alive and that he was OK. The man's name was Mr. Wagner, and he had Alzheimer's. I called Shelbyville and told them who I was. I talked to Detective Reed, a member of the Sheriff's department who was in charge of the case.

I offered to come down and help look for Mr. Wagner, who was still missing the next day. My boyfriend and I drove down there and met with Detective Reed. I'll never forget what he said to me the morning we met. He sat across his desk from me, and said," I've busted more psychics than I can count. If you're not the real thing, get up and leave now. Don't waste my time and yours."

When I didn't get up to leave, he just looked at me. I started telling him what I had seen in connection with Mr. Wagner, and it went from there. After a while, he asked me if I would meet with the family and talk to them. This is something

I don't like to do, but I will if asked to. I don't like to be the one to tell a family that a loved one is dead. I don't think that's my job, but I will if I must.

I met with the family and talked to them. They had a cap of his and asked if it would help me to find him. I told them it might, and they went and got it for me. At first, I thought that I was picking on someone else, and asked them if someone else had been wearing the cap. They said no, just Mr. Wagner. I couldn't understand it. I was receiving clear images, but I got the feeling the timing was wrong. I didn't know the area at all and that didn't help.

I started describing what I was seeing, but no one seemed to know what I was talking about. This made me wonder if I was going to be able to help them. I could see a house, and a white barn beside it; I could feel a pond or a creek close by. Then one of the women asked me to describe the house again, she said she needed to make a phone call. A moment later she came back and said that she knew now where I was talking about. She had called a family member in Ohio, and that had been the house he had grown up in. I couldn't understand why I would be picking up this house, but when I told them about the woman I saw on the front porch, she looked at me and said, "That was me when we first got married."

I remembered that he had Alzheimer's, and everything fell into place. I was picking up what he was thinking. He believed that he still lived there and was trying to go home to Ohio. That was why he left, thinking he was going home to see his wife. That was where he thought he should be. His mind was gone completely, and I had to think of a way to get around it.

I took the cap in my hands and opened my mind to him. I had to see what him was around, but not through his eyes. I had been trying that and it hadn't worked. One of the biggest problems I find is having to depend on the police to know where it is I'm seeing. In a place like Shelbyville, Tennessee there are mostly farms. Most of the farmers have silos for one thing or another, and I knew that wouldn't help me.

I could see Mr. Wagner sitting in a tree line. He was alive at that time because I could see him moving. Over the tops of the trees, I saw a large white house off in the distance. It sat back to the right from where he was. I could see the roof of the house and knew that it wasn't a standard roof, but that was all I could see. It was up to them to find this house. I knew the locals would know the house I was talking about.

We went back to the Sheriff's office, and I thought that would be the end of it. Before I left Detective Reed asked me if I could tell him anything about another case he was working on. By now I felt comfortable working with him and said I would try. I must admit after what he said at the beginning; I was ready to get back a little of my own.

I sat across from his desk again, and we talked. He held a file of some kind in his hand. Before he could say anything, I started describing the murder scene to him. He hadn't shown me the file; I was just taking it from his mind. He stopped talking and just looked at me. I laughed and asked him if he thought I was real now or not. We laughed about it, and he asked me how I knew what the murder scene looked like. I told him that was my job, remember I was a psychic. He laughed and spoke "You have me on that one".

I could see an elderly lady and how she was lying on the floor, and which way her head was facing. I told him what her house looked like, and what was around it. It was great to see the look on his face, and know he now believed that I was the real thing, not just someone calling myself a psychic. I described the killer's physical appearance and his clothing. I could also see what kind of car he drove. I told him where I saw the murderer weapon, and who I saw put it there. I never learned the elderly lady's name, but then I don't need a name to work a case. Later he referred me to another sheriff's department that he thought I might need my help. I kept in touch with him until he left the department for places unknown. I do know that he teaches now, but not where.

One place he referred me to was Fayetteville, Tennessee. They got in touch with me about a woman who was missing. They called and talked to me, and I told them I would try to help if I could. The next day they came and picked me up. The officer's name was Joyce McConnell. After I arrived at the Sheriff's office, I met the sheriff whose name was Ray Rhoton. He was a big man with a smile that matched his size.

That was one case in which I learned something about myself. We started leaving the office, so they could show me where they thought the body was. Just as we were pulling out of the parking lot, I saw a Bronco drive by. I knew it wasn't really but couldn't understand why it was there. I could see through it. I had never had this happen to me before, but I knew there had to be a reason why I was being shown this.

I looked at Joyce and said, "Follow that Bronco". She looked around us, then back at me. "Where"? I told her the one in front of us. By now I'm used to seeing images, but not like this. Usually, it's people I see this way. I didn't know what else to tell her, but to follow it. I didn't know if it would disappear or not. I didn't think about how it sounded to her. I told her she couldn't see it, just turn when I told her to. Afterward she told me she really thought she had a good one in the car that time. Here she was following something she couldn't see, taking the word of someone she had just met. It was her first time working with a psychic and she didn't know what to expect.

I hadn't been expecting this either, but I didn't tell her this. She turned where I told her to, and we followed the Bronco down one road after another. I could see a man and a woman in the front seat of the Bronco but had no idea who they were. I knew that whenever the woman turned her head to look out the window, I could see what it was she was seeing. As we drove, I told her there's an old barn coming up, and it would be just as I had seen it the eyes of the woman in the Bronco. Joyce asked if I knew where we were going, I told her I had no idea, that I had never been to Fayetteville before. That I didn't know one road from another

When we came to a "y" in the road, I told her to stop. I could see the people in the Bronco just sitting there. Finally, they turned to the right. She asked me why I wanted to go that way, I told her because that was the way they had gone after hesitating briefly, she turned the car to the right. I Finally I told her to stop at a small white house and turn into the drive. She asked my why, and I laughed and said," They went in there".

She said she couldn't. I didn't ask why, because she knew where she could go, and I didn't. She turned to me in the car, and asked if I knew the people who lived in the white house. I told her no, that it was just where the Bronco turned in. I didn't know anyone in town but the people I had met at the sheriff's office. "Are you sure?" she asked me again. I knew then that it had to have something to do with the case.

She told me then that the resident of this white house was related to the man they suspected of doing the killing. This was where she had been meaning to take me. She asked if I could describe the Bronco and I said yes. I told her what I had seen, and what the Bronco had looked like to me. I didn't tell her that I had been able to see through it. She really would have thought I had gone around the bend. I had done all I could do; it was now up to the sheriff's office to do the rest. I had no jurisdiction on anyone's property, so I had to sit on the sidelines, which was fine with me. If they went back to look, I have no idea; my job was over, and I returned home.

While I was there, I talked to them about a few more of the cases they were working on. I didn't get into them to deeply but told them all I could.

One I looked at for them was about a boy who had been accused of shooting his father. This time Joyce took me through muddy cornfields and down to a small creek. By the time we got there, I was tired. When I work on a case, I don't just sit around and do it; I go wherever they need me to go.

When we got there, she asked me what I could tell her. I opened up my mind and looked to the past. I saw a family of three standing by the water. I could see a man down by the edge of the creek and a woman standing behind him with a gun. For some reason they had been told that the boy had killed the father, but I could see the woman doing it. I could see her shoot him in the back of the head, and him fall over in the creek. I could see the boy standing back away from them crying. I told her what I saw, and she said she would tell the sheriff. I walked around for a minute and sensed the location of the gun. I could see her put it in the trailer she was using to move with. By then I told them it was out of the state, and I didn't think they would find it. They told me she had used a small trailer to move to North Carolina and was no longer living in Tennessee.

One was a floater. That's a body they pulled out of the water. They asked me if I could tell them anything about him. I had never seen one before, but I'm used to about anything, and I can handle a lot. The remains looked like it had been a human being at one time, but after being in the water for so long it made me wonder.

I've been back down there a few times since then; I had friends there and drop by to see them occasionally. I told them I would be back, that there would be a murder of a child and I would be back. I did, and the day I was there they found a child murdered in a cornfield. These are the times I wish I was wrong, and that I had never been born with this gift. I can handle the bodies of adults, but children get to me badly. It has to be a very sick person to kill a child, but when its their own it's even worse. A child is a gift from God, not something you kill and leave in a cornfield. I was standing there when they brought the stuff in from the child's murder. It hit me like someone taking their fist and hitting me between the eyes. I could see the man who did it and told them what he looked like. I told them it was the father, that he had done this. Later he confessed. I knew that he had done it, and I knew he would go to jail, knowing that he would pay was the only thing that would help me get through it.

One case I worked on was in Henderson, Kentucky. I worked with the Kentucky State Police with this one. A woman had been taken from there by gunpoint neither she or her body couldn't be found. No one had heard from her since the day she was seen been abducted.

This was like all cases I work on; I don't want to know anything about it. That's the first thing I tell them. I sat across from the detective and told him what I could about the killer; I told him that the killer lived in a trailer, and what I could see around it. I told him the killer had a beard, and that he had a drinking problem, maybe even a drug problem. At first, I couldn't figure out why I wasn't picking him up stronger than I was; then I realized he was dead. I told that to the Detective and told him I would help find the body if I could.

I could see an open field behind where the body was. I could also see a house back off to the right in the field. I didn't see it but could feel a pond or a lake close by. I could see it over to the left of where I was seeing this. There was a drain of some kind. There was a big dip in the ground, and a covered well sticking up from the ground. I couldn't see the body, not all of it anyway. It looked to me like parts of the body were gone. I held the picture of the missing girl in my hand and knew that what I was seeing was where her body was or had been. I could see leaves from the trees covering the ground. I drew them a picture of what I was seeing. It took two days to find the place I had seen. When we got there, there was nobody, but you could tell something had been there. It had been a while since she had been missing. I don't know how long, but I knew it was over a month. The only thing that could have happened was animals had gotten to the body.

We knew the guy I had envisioned did not come back to get the body, because he had killed himself after they had questioned him about her, so there was no other explanation. They said they would bring the cadaver dogs in, but the next week there was a big snow. I don't know if they ever did go back. I had done all I could do. It was up to them now to find her body.

Another case that I worked on was the Lora Cecere case. She was a soldier stationed at Fort Campbell, Kentucky. Her disappearance had been reported in the newspaper and on television. On this case I waited awhile before saying anything to anyone, because I thought they would find the body. A few months later when they hadn't, I called Detective Lilis, with whom I had worked I had worked on several cases and told him what I had seen. This was in January of 97. A few months later, the media were still reporting her as missing.

When I called back the second time, I knew that I would never be able to just let this one go. Somehow, I had picked up on Lora's spirit very strongly, she was there with me. I could see her in my mind at times. Then there were the times it seemed like she was there with me. I would see her in my dreams telling me not to stop, that she needed my help. I would be working around my house, doing this or that, and she would seem to just show up. I would stop what I was doing and tell her I needed her help as well.

The first time I saw her in a vision, she was standing beside the road pointing at something. I could see her mouth moving as if she were trying to tell me something. There was a tree line behind her, but that wasn't what she was pointing at. I could see an electric tower by her, and what looked like to me a round white tower behind her to the left. I knew from the feelings I was getting that she wasn't in Hopkinsville, but that she was close by. I couldn't see the white tower well enough to see if there was any kind of writing on it or what kind it was. I drew what I could of the vision I was getting. I drove everyone I knew crazy asking them it they knew where this place was. I would ask them if they knew what kind of tower it was in the picture. I knew that I hadn't seen one like it anywhere close to where I lived.

With me sometimes visions can be like puzzles. I get one piece at a time. I may see the same thing repeatedly, or it might have something added the next time I see it. This was what was happening in this case. I would see something, and then the next time it would be a little longer. It was like watching a movie and just being able to watch a little more each time. I told Lora that I needed more to go on, that I could not find her just by what she was showing me. I didn't even know where to start looking.

A few days later I started seeing a road I knew well, it was Wilma Rudolph Boulevard, in Clarksville. About eleven miles from where I lived. I had been on this road dozens of times going to the mall in Clarksville. This road also led to Guthrie, Kentucky, a few miles north of the mall.

I could see a truck going down the road, and I could feel Lora in the truck. From where I was standing, I could see the road well, and knew the truck was headed away from the mall. What was driving me crazy was just as it went under the interstate 24 overpass near the mall, I would lose her. This drove me nuts trying to figure out where the truck went after it went under the over pass. I told my sister Polly I had to go look, because the feeling I was receiving, the truck shouldn't have just stopped. I asked her if she would go with me, and she said yes.

We drove up to Wilma Rudolph Boulevard and stopped just off exit 4. I waited to see if I would pick up the truck again, planning to follow it. I but told Polly I wanted to see what happened if I stopped just under the overpass where I always lost them. I drove up and stopped. I waited for a minute and then went on. Just beyond the overpass, was a gas station. I had to drive past it to turn around. Just as I passed it, I lost the feeling of Lora's presence. I knew then that I had passed wherever she had been last on this road.

I turned around and went back. Just before I passed the gas station again, my sister said," There's a road beside the station". I hadn't seen it the first time, and probably wouldn't have that time if she hadn't said something. It was just a little road that went back behind the gas station and veered to the right. I turned onto the road, not knowing where it would take me. I had never been back here before and didn't know what I was going to find. The little road curved this way and that, with woods on each side. About a mile or so down the road, it cleared out. There was an industrial park back there.

I could feel Lora more strongly now than I had on the main road. I knew she was back there but didn't know where. We drove on down the road looking for a place to turn around, because I knew I had passed Lora again. Her body was somewhere along that road, but I hadn't seen anything she had showed me. As we drove back, going the other way, I hit my brakes. There I could see everything that I was looking for. I didn't see it from the other direction because it was on the other side of the road. I told Polly, "This is it". This is the spot Lora showed me in the vision. It was all there, the electric tower and the round white tower in the back off to the left. The field I had seen her in, pointing to the tower was there also. I just needed now to find her.

I got out of my car and walked to where I had seen Lora standing. I looked around and knew I would never be able to find her myself in this area. It was larger in real life than it had looked in the vision. There was a little dirt road that led from the road into a field. You could tell it had been driven on in the last few weeks. It was hot and I didn't want to step on any snakes, so I went back to the car. I told Polly I would call just as soon as I got back home. I would have to wait because this was one case that had been passed around from one police department to another so many times, I couldn't keep up with who had it. It had gone from Oak Grove, Kentucky police to Hopkinsville then to Clarksville police, then to the Army CID. No one seemed to know who it belonged to. Finally, it ended up with the Army (CID).

I went back and called Detective. Lilies and he said he would call around to find out whom I should contact. Well in that time I had been on the phone to a friend of mine who knew someone in Cadiz, Kentucky who had cadaver dogs. The man with the dogs was named Jim Gray. He told me yes; he would be willing to take his dogs down there and have a look. He and his wife Carrie called friends of theirs and by the time the day came to go down to the field in Clarksville, a dozen people had appeared with dogs from all over the US. Someone had gotten permission to go onto the land to look. Channel 43 News from here in Hopkinsville had gotten wind of it and was also there. I had never worked with cadaver dogs before and didn't 't know what to expect.

We called the Clarksville police and told them what we had found; they told us we would have to call CID. I got on the phone and talked to them and told them what we had found. Need to say they never got back with me. I would call and call until I could talk to someone. At one time we thought about going up there and doing the digging but were told we couldn't.

In the meantime, a jawbone was sent to Channel 43 News. The letter sent along with the jawbone, stated that it was Lora Cecere's jawbone. The crime lab confirmed this that was when they finally gave up hope of finding her alive.

I was told to let them take it from there. Well, it's 1998 now, and still Lora's body has not been found. I have talked to her mother a few times on the phone and have met with her for coffee. I have done all I can do, but I will never give up hope that she will be found. I will continue to offer my help if there is a chance that she can be found, even if it takes ten years or more.

Since the Lora Cerece case, I have been contacted about other cases, but at this time I can't go into them. They are still under investigation, and anything I might say could hurt the case. I don't know when, maybe tomorrow but if I feel that I can be of help to anyone with a missing person or murder case I will offer my services.

I have called the authorities on cases and received returned callers on several occasions. One was in Nashville, Tennessee. There had been a little girl murdered and they were looking for her body. I could see it beside a small road, and I could see a man walking away from it. I could see him clearly and knew what he looked like. I called Nashville and told them what I had seen, and they called me back. I gave them what I had picked up, told them what the man had looked like. They never called back, but when they found the killer, it was the man I had described to them. I met him the minute I saw him. I didn't call back because as far as I was concerned, they had the right man.

On some murder cases I have used other means besides my psychic ability. I sometimes use a pendulum for finding a body. I have used one for quite a few years. I find that when I need to narrow something down on a map, I use it. It helps me to know in what direction at least to start looking.

You can buy one where they sell Tarot Cards and books about psychics. I put mine on a gold chain and always keep it with me. I carry it with a crystal to keep it pure, I know this sounds strange, but it works. This way it doesn't carry anything over from one case to another.

I have used it for finding lost objects even around my house. Once you use one long enough you get to the point that it works the minute you pick it up. First, it's best to let it get used to you. I know this sounds funny, but if you want it to work well for you this is best. Hold it in your hand and let it pick up your vibes. This way it will know you from others.

To use it on a map you must first ask it what you want to know. This doesn't have to be out loud; it can be in your mind. But make sure it can be answered in a yes or no fashion. It will help to learn the movement of yes and no when you first buy it. Then when it works, you will understand it.

On a map I start out with "is the body in this area?" and go from there. I then break it down using a grid. I go from one side of a map to the other until I find what I'm looking for. If you have a large area map this can be done by asking it to be shown in which direction the body is. Then go the way it shows you. The closer it gets the body the faster and smaller the circle gets. Then at that point it will just about stop altogether, as if to get right over the body.

I have had them go nuts on me, but its only happens when there is more than one body picked up at that point. This can be very disheartening at times because you don't understand what is going on. After you use your pendulum for a while this slows down.

Pendulums can be used for other things such as dousing water. This is what most people use them for, but after you learn how to use them, they can be used for almost anything. I have used it to look for gas and water underneath the ground. I can't tell you if this is unusual or not. I never heard of anyone using it for that, but with me it works.

Visions

People hear about psychic vision but may not understand what the term means in relation to the psychic realm. With different psychics it can mean several different things. With me, psychic visions come in different forms and usually at the wrong times. Some visions can be thought of as a dream or they may come while I'm wide wake. They may also come as images in my mind. Either way they can be very upsetting, or just plain funny. If I had my choice, I would take the funny ones any day. Not that I have a choice.

People ask me how I see things when I have a vision and if I can do it at will. I tell them yes, that most of the time I can. The reason for this is that since the earlier days, I have had more control over it. I have learned to shut most of it out of my mind when I am doing something else. The very strong ones seem to have a mind of their own. I can't push them to the back of my mind or turn them off. The best way to describe it is "a wall you put up in your mind". This wall is to block out everything that tries to sneak in while I'm not thinking about it. I have to do this because if I didn't, I would live in the other world all the time, and I wouldn't be able to function in this one at all. The reason for this is because the other world can be stronger than the real world sometimes. The visions that come to me can be so strong that they will block out everything else around me. What I am driving in a car, or cooking supper doesn't have any meaning when it comes to having a vision.

Sometimes pictures just pop into my head and stay there. I find those to be the worst ones. Once they're there, there is not much you can do about them. Once you've seen something, you can't very well "not see it". It's there whether you like it or not. This doesn't happen to me often, but it does happen. Once it's there I must follow it through, or it drives me crazy. It will keep popping up until I admit it's there. I must stop what I'm doing and go over it. These have caught me when I'm working or talking to someone. I could be cleaning my house, and it hits me. People around me at that time just stare at me, wondering if I'm OK. After it's over if I'm alone I just go about whatever I was doing at the time. If not, I usually must stop and tell people what's happening. I don't won't people to think that I'm having blackout are losing my mind.

I can say that there have been times that they are so funny I have had to stop what I was doing because I was laughing so hard. These are the ones I don't really mind. They can be hard to take at times though. I have these sometimes after

I spend the day with someone, and still have them on my mind. I get pictures of them in my mind, and they may be doing something that I think is funny. Later I told them about it and they would say, “I thought no one was looking”. It can be anything from falling on their butt to just saying the wrong thing. I know people don’t like to be caught at moments they feel will make them look foolish, and I really can’t help it. I don’t do it because I want to. It’s because I ‘m still tuned into them from being around them that day or talking to them on the phone. I don’t know if other psychics experience this kind of thing, but I know I go through them quite often.

Mostly I get the one that takes me by surprise when I have my mind on something I’m working on. If I have a vision while working on a case, I write it down in detail, and go on. Then later I go back and try to make some sense of what I have written down. Sometimes this works and sometimes it doesn’t. It’s like getting a puzzle with lots of pieces missing and trying to make sense of the one you do have. I have the hardest time with the ones that just pop in and out of my mind quickly. I just get pieces and nothing else. I may see a body lying on the ground or the floor, and not know if the person is dead or alive and it doesn’t last long enough for me know. This can drive me crazy because I’m left wondering about what it pertains to. Am I seeing a case where I will be working in the future or am I just picking up something this happened in the past. By this I mean the boy I'm seeing that was lying in the vicinity of where I'm at some point in time. This can be really confusing not only to me, but when I give the police some information. I do let them know that it was just a quick insight, and that I don't know if it pertains to the case are not.

I try to keep files on the cases I work in; this way I can keep them separate. I don't need them to get mixed up. It would be disastrous. Some time I use a notebook for each case and just write them down as they happen. When the case is over, I put the notebook away until or if I need it later. Sometimes I am asked about a case later and must go back to these files to look up something, and this way I'll have them.

If a bad vision catches me unaware, I have been known to drop dishes I'm washing or a cup of coffee that I have my hand at the time. I try to stop wherever I am and let it pass before doing anything. If I'm driving down the road, I try to pullover as soon as possible and wait it out. I sometimes lean against the wall until it passes if I get lucky. This I found to be safer for everyone involved. While writing this book it has happened more than once, and I have had to stop. Because I have my mind on this, the visions seem to sneak up on me quite often. I have had to stop everything and go do something else. Sometimes I even lay down when this happens.

Visions

I really have a hard time with visions that come as dreams. You have no control over your subconscious, so I can't hold them back. They're there no matter what. When I wake up, they are as clear as if I had let them in. This is very upsetting to a psychic because no one likes not having control over their minds and body. Even if you know it can happen, you still don't like it.

I have found that when this happens in my sleep it sometimes goes farther than I would like. I have even had what I call "out of body experiences". Those are the worst for me to deal with. Being asleep in bed, and knowing your mind leaves your body, going someplace that you don't know, is hard to understand for someone who has never had it happen to them. You think of your mind and body as one, working together to make you one person. This is not always how it works for me. Being psychic, I can't stop this from happening if there is away, I haven't found it. After you get to the point I am at, with my abilities, you just learn to live with it, at least I do. You would think that as a psychic you should be able to do it or stop whenever you want to. This is not the case for me. My psychic abilities have gotten strong enough that they sometimes will out. If I just had one to worry about, I think I could control it. But with more than one or two, they seem to get to me one way or another. I can't seem to fight all of them off at once, so I just try to keep the ones that pop up the most from ruling me. This is something I have had to learn to do.

This happened to me in the "Maxie case". I went to bed as I usually do, with nothing on my mind that I knew of. I could not have heard of Maxie, because he wasn't even known by the police or the media at that time. I didn't know him in my personal life either or at work. As far as I know, I had never even met this man before that night. This is why this took me by surprise and even frightened me to some extent.

I remember laying down about ten o'clock that night. My sister in others and I in the family had all been sitting around drinking coffee and talking. Not about anything, just a normal conversation about people we know and things that were happening. The kids were telling me about school and some of their friends, and Polly in I were talking about the factory where she worked. No one had mentioned anything spooky or scary or told anything about anyone dying. There was nothing mentioned that would trigger this kind of experience. I knew I had worked the next day, and I knew I had to get to bed soon if I wanted to get up in time the next morning. I remember telling everybody good night and leaving them at the table in the dining room.I took a bath and got into pajamas and crawled in bed just like any other night. I was so tired I must have been asleep the minute my head hit the pillow.

I do know that at the time I woke up, I didn't feel like a normally would when I got up in the morning. It was kind of like when you just open your eyes and you're awake. This is nothing unusual for me, I'm one of those people the minute my eyes open I'm awake and ready for the day. I knew the minute that I opened my eyes something was different, something was wrong. Then I told myself I was just having a dream that I would really wake up any moment and I would be back in my bed. But this time I was wrong.

Not knowing where you are or why you're there is the hardest part to understand. If you knew where you were, and could recognize the things around you, it wouldn't be so hard to take in.   It's like being asleep and someone moving you out of your house into one you don't know, then waking up not knowing where you are.

When I "popped" into the house I was in the living room. I knew I had never seen the room or either of the people there. At first, I didn't know why I was there, or where I was. I was in a strange person's home, not knowing how I got there. I had no idea what was going on. I could see everything around me, as if I were really standing in the room with the two occupants in the room with me. Glancing around me I could see the flowers hanging from a hanging planter on the wall above the woman's head that was sitting in the chair. Seeing a hallway that led off into another unfamiliar room and into a nearby room that I recognized as the kitchen. In the room I was in I could even see the pattern of the couch that sat against the far wall. I could imagine where I was because I knew I hadn't walked in the front door as you normally would; I was just there.

I began to realize that I seemed to be floating, and that I couldn't feel my body. That's what I began to believe, that I was peeking through a hole in the wall, watching these two people I didn't know. I knew I was seeing out of my own eyes, but I couldn't feel my body. I could hear voices but couldn't hear them clearly enough to distinguish the words. It sounded to me as in they were mumbling, in low voices. The one thing I did hear was her scream. When this happened, it seemed as if someone had poured a bucket of ice water on me. I felt a cold chill come over my body that went all the way down to my toes. I had never felt anything like it in my life. I know it's nothing like you feel when you hear someone one television scream. The sound of screaming at the moment of death is indescribable. There is nothing that I know of to compare it with.

When the man turned from where the woman sat in the chair, I could see her clearly then, I seem to be standing not more than three or four feet away from her. The man moved away from her as he took a step back from the woman in the chair. At that moment I knew this wasn't a dream it was more of a nightmare. I could see what looked like blood covering the front of the woman's nightgown. For a moment I didn't understand what was happening. The red seems to spread rapidly across the front of her. It was then that I could see the gaping wounds in her throat. It took me a second to realize that he had cut her throat, and just turned away. As he turned around, he stood facing me, not more than three feet away. It seemed as if he were staring me right in the eye. He stood for a minute and then walked on.

The only thought in my mind right then was he might start for me next. I couldn't move and didn't know how to stop what was happening. Then I realized why he hadn't said anything to me, or tried to touch me, he couldn't see me. My body wasn't there in the room, just my mind. He didn't know I was there and had no idea I was watching him. After I realized this, it helped me get through it, because I could take in the details of the room. For some reason I knew I needed to know what every detail of the room and that the murderer looked like.

I didn't know at the time that what I was seeing was real. As I said I thought it was a nightmare I was having, just as everyone else does. I didn't know then that I had just been a witness to a real murder. I just knew for some unknown reason I had to know everything I could about the room I was in, even down to the color of the walls and carpet. I didn't realize at the time I would be getting myself in the middle of a major homicide investigation. I just knew that I had to absorb every detail I could see.

I couldn't see where he went because I couldn't turn around from where I stood. I couldn't move around the room either. The only thing that I could see was what was in front of me now, and that was the woman sitting in the chair dying. Knowing there's nothing you can do and that there's no way to help someone in this position is the hardest thing a person can go through. I knew the woman was dying before my eyes at I could do a thing to help her. The next morning when I woke up, I could remember everything that happened the night before. I didn't know how or why I did, I just knew that it was very clear in my mind. I didn't know if I should tell anyone because I didn't know if it had been real or not. I have had nightmares before, but with this one seems so real it was unnerving.

This kind of thing had never happened to me before an I didn't know how to take it. I had had visions before, but not like this one. Being out of my body like that was very unsettling. It was like nothing I had ever experienced before, and I can't say that even now when it happens that I'm really any better at knowing what's going on or why when I open my eyes. I still feel as if I'm peeking in on someone. That feeling is something that I don't think I'll ever get used to. Thank God this doesn't happen to me too often, because I don't like the feeling it leaves behind.

There are some that say they can teach you how to do this at will. I don't know if this is true, but I wouldn't if I didn't have to. Just from the feelings I get when this happens, I wouldn't do it willingly. I know that sounds strange, but it's true. Not being in control is not easy. I have had other psychics tell me that I should be able to control it, and not let it control me. They don't seem to understand that with as many abilities as I have, you can't control all of them at one time. I know this is hard for them to understand because as I've said before most psychics don't have as many abilities as I do and can have some control over what's happening. I 'm a believer in the old saying "you better watch what you wish for". I say this because I've had psychics as well as someone who isn't psychic, people tell me they wish they could leave their bodies.

This has happened one other time that I care to remember. I can't say that I don't have any control at all. because I do. When asked to do readings for people, I can open my mind to see the past as well as the future. I don't mind doing it because I can stop these kinds of visions when I feel the need. I can investigate someone' s life and see the people who mean the most to them, and the things that go on in their everyday life. I see their lives as pictures or as if I were watching a video, some time's I can see parts and sections of their houses a know something is happening at that place, sometimes it's just bits and pieces.

The one thing I'm not good at is age. When I see someone in a vision, I can't tell age to well. Sometimes it's because I don't get a good look at them, or I just get a vague image. Ever in real life some of us have a hard time telling someone's age. In today's world with so many things out on the market to help slow the aging process, all of us have a hard time. What I do get is an idea about what decade they are in, like if they are in their twenties or thirties, or so on. Most of the time I get an image of the face or a body, but not enough to tell anything about.

I do see hair color, and most of the time I get a feeling of eye color. I can tell the size (slim or heavy set) and I can see what kind of clothes they wear, or if they are wearing a hat. I can see race, and sex of the person. If they have a scar or a tattoo, I may be able to pick this up. I may not see scars, but I can tell what part of the body it is on. I may see the kind of car they drive or at least know the color range or the size. Sometimes I can see the house they live in. Sometimes I get lucky and can see the outside of their house. But mostly it's just rooms they are in. Most of the time I can pick up on children that they may have. If I see someone being hurt, I try to tell the police about it to describe the person to them.

When Bob Rascoe, a friend of mine came for a reading once, I could see him hurting himself. I could tell it would be with wood and doing something in the ground. I couldn't see it all. I just saw him outside working with his hands. I could see him in my mind bending over as if he were in pain. Two months later he got his finger cut off driving wooden fence posts into the ground. I told him once that I saw him hurting his knee and told him to watch for snakes. A week later he twisted his knee trying to keep from stepping on a snake.

I started out reading for Bob when someone gave him my name and address. He came in and sat down. He started asking me questions and I would answer them. Then I looked at him and said, "Now it's my turn". I'll never forget his face when I started telling him about a pipe that was sticking out from a wall in his house. I had never been to his house and didn't know where he even lived. He just sat there looking at me. I then told him about a sinkhole coming in the yard. He went home and found it where I told him it would be. After that, we became good friends.

I will say I have been incorrect a time or two or at least off on my timing. Once I had the feeling that something very bad was going to happen. This is how my visions start out sometimes as just a bad feeling that keeps getting worse. Then my visions start to manifest as something I will see that's not there. This is how this vision started out. I didn't know what it was, but I knew it would affect the whole town of Hopkinsville where I lived. I stepped out of my house and stopped dead in my tracks. The whole street in front of my house was filled with something I couldn't quite make out. I just knew that whatever it was, wasn't supposed to be there. I didn't get a clean picture of what it was, but I could see shapes. I knew that whatever it wasn't man made. After a minute it cleared up, and the street was back to normal. I didn't know what it was I was supposed to see, but I knew it was very bad. I could feel myself about to cry and I didn't know why. Calling somebody wasn't an option. I didn't know what to tell them I was seeing. I just felt sorry for the people around me, and what they had to go through. I couldn't understand this because I didn't know them well enough to know what was happening in their lives. I just knew it had something to do with what I was seeing.

This bothered me for more than a month. I couldn't bring myself to say anything to anyone but Bob and my sister. They both said I should tell someone about what I had seen. I didn't know what I had seen, so how could I tell anyone? I thought it best I kept it to myself. About a week later I was driving in downtown Hopkinsville and was just about to cross a bridge and I could see water coming up at me. It was rising so fast I couldn't get away from it. I hit my brakes in the car and slid about fifteen feet.

When the car came to a stop, I looked but couldn't see any water anywhere. The river wasn't up, and I couldn't understand it. That was the second time in one day this had happened to me. There was no explaining it. I just sat there wondering what to do. I didn't know where to call or what to tell them if I did call someone. What was I going to tell them, that the water in the river seemed to come up at me? They would have had me carted away.

I thought about it some more until I started getting headaches from worrying about it. This was in late 1996, in December. I broke down and called DES here in Hopkinsville and talked to them. I told them what I had seen, and who to call the police department. That way they would know who I am. I told them that I could see water and other stuff covering the road on North Drive, close to my house. I could also see the water coming up over the riverbank downtown. I told them for some reason February stuck in my mind as to when it would happen. And I gave them a day. I told them that they needed to make sure that the water, that I could see in different parts of town covered with water didn't cut them off. I told them it could be anything from a flood to a tornado. I didn't know just what it was, but that I could not keep quiet about it any longer.

February was just about over, and nothing happened. There had been a psychic a few years before that said Kentucky and this region was going to have an earthquake. This had scared half the people in Hopkinsville to death, and I didn't want this to happen again, so I kept quiet.

At the end of February 1997 Hopkinsville had the worse flood since 1967. Houses were lost and roads were closed. North Drive was flooded and so was the river where I had seen it come over its banks at me that day. I can say I was wrong about the year; it happened a year later than I had thought it would, but I hit it right on the day and the month that it happened.

This was one time I really wished I had been wrong, all together. I saw people I knew without homes, and houses with water up past the roofs. This hit me hard. These are the things that happen, and knowing there is not one thing you can do to stop it doesn't make it any better. I felt that being psychic was useless sometimes, and knowing something is going to happen and not being able to stop it is like being an engineer on a runaway freight train.

Sometimes I think I'm a danger to myself as well as my family. There are times that I can be doing something like cooking or taking a bath when I just seem to go off into another world. My family knows this look; they have seen it many times. I'm glad I don't have to see it because hearing about it is bad enough. I have been told I look like someone on drugs, and I don't even take aspirin if I can help it.

For example, I was sitting at my sister's playing cards with her and friends. When it came my turn, I just sat there. As I said, my sister knows this look. She calls it "The lights are on and no body's home look". I seem to stare off at something unknown, and just sit there. She says my eyes seem to look like they turn to blue glass, and I never blink, that I just start talking.

She knows to grab a pen and paper and write down whatever I say, even if it makes no sense. There is no trying to talk to me or get me out of it until I'm ready. I don't feel your touch or hear your voice. I just sit there like a zombie, and everybody must wait. I don't do this because I want to; this is just something that happens. There is never any telling what I will say, or about what.

This usually happens right before a case. I may get a vision of a case that is coming up, or of a case I'm in now. I have to wait and see. This can be very upsetting because if it's a case I've not heard about or know nothing about, I feel lost. I just must set it aside and wait until something happens.

I know when this happens to look for details. I look at everybody in the vision, and make sure that I can describe them. I also look at houses or cars, and the clothes they may be wearing. If I see a child in my vision I pay special attention to them, so I will know them when the time comes.

The only problem with this is that this may happen more than once in a day. If I'm playing cards or doing something that should have my attention, I stop and just wait. It may not happen but once, but I don't want to be doing something that I could just tune off. Like cooking. I'm scared I could catch the house on fire. I know this sounds like I need a keeper, but I'm fine.

The reason I know that I don't have control over this is once I drove down interstate I-24 for ten miles like this. I was driving the guy I was dating at the time to Nashville to the V. A. Hospital. We were talking and listening to the radio. The next thing I knew we were ten miles down the road from where the vision started. I had been driving sixty-five miles an hour this way.

I could see my oldest son with nurses and doctors around him. He was talking OK, but they had him on a gurney, and I could see blood. I could hear the doctors asking him questions and checking his arms and legs for broken bones. I could tell he was OK, but I didn't know what had happened. I waited to see if they did anything other than that, and when they didn't, I seemed to come out of it. My boyfriend didn't know what to do. I don't know what would have happened if he had touched me. This is one thing that has never happened. Most of the time I'm alone or someone else is there and knows not to touch me, but they watch me until it's over. This time I was driving, and he didn't want to scare me, and make me have a wreck. He stayed very alert and ready to take the wheel for me if he needed t

When I came out of it, he asked what had happened. I told him what I saw, and he went crazy. He made me stop the car and let him drive, which I thought at the time was a good idea. I don't know what would have happened it he had touched me or tried to get me to stop. I had never done this before while driving a car.

It didn't happen again while we were gone to Nashville, but it did when I returned to Hopkinsville. I was sitting watching television and just blanked out. I could see this time that the doctors and nurses were trying to make him lie down, and they were giving him a shot. I couldn't tell anything else about it; it just went away. This time I knew it would happen soon; I didn't know why but I did. I knew there was no reason to get upset, that everything would be fine, but this was my son, and I didn't like that waiting.

That night my nephew and his family had decided to move from the house they lived in. They were driving at night with the children in the back of the truck, to pick up another load, of furniture and someone pulled it out in front of them. The boys in the back got knocked around and one of my sons fell out. I was called to the hospital to the ER where they had been taken. There were the doctors and nurses I had seen in my vision. They were all there. Dominic wasn't hurt, but he needed a shot, because of scrapes and cuts. I knew that everything would be OK; I had seen it that day. But it never stops a mother from worrying.

It happened when everything turned out fine, my oldest daughter Christy was going to have a baby and we were sitting around the kitchen talking about it. I had bought a little chair for the baby, even though it would be a while before the baby would be used. I was washing dishes and turned to where Christy was sitting. There on the floor beside her was a little girl with black curly hair and big brown eyes, sitting in the chair I had just bought. She looked up at me and smiled. I told Christy that her baby was sitting right in front of her and that I could see her.

Christy stood up and looked around and asked, "Why can't I see her?" I told her that she would soon, that she would just have to wait. About five months later, Christy had a beautiful baby girl and named her Anjel Salina. She had a head full of black hair and had the biggest brown eyes you've ever seen. She was beautiful. Christy says I think that way because she's my first grandchild, she may have a point there.

I have had visions that stopped me in my tricks. Once when I received a vision of fire and children, I could see someplace burning, but couldn't tell where it was. I could see children all around it, but not enough to know if it was someone's home or not. Finally, I sat down and opened my mind up to it. I needed to know what was burning. I had to know more about it. When it involves children, I pay closer attention to it.

The vision became clearer after a moment. I didn't know which one it was, but I did know it was here in Hopkinsville. I called the police and told them what I had seen, and how I knew it was here in town. The feeling was so close to me that I thought it might have been my son's school at the time.

The next day Highland school caught on fire. No children were in the building, but they were to go to school the next day. I wish I could have told them which school it was that was going to catch fire, but I couldn't. A lot of the schools have undergone changes since I went to them. I had gone to Highland as a child, but a lot of work has been done since then, and I didn't recognize it.

I have had visions that my family told me not to get in because they thought it wasn't safe. I know they mean well, but sometimes it just isn't that easy. One of those times was when there was a murder of two women. I could see them being murdered. I was sitting watching television and it just hit me. I could see a fast-food restaurant, but not what kind. I knew that the man doing the killing was just passing through, that he didn't live in Hopkinsville or Clarksville. I could see him standing talking to the women at the counter, and then pulling out a gun. I could see him making them walk out of the building and get into a car. I came out of it then and didn't see anything else.

I hadn't heard about any murders in town or in Clarksville, so I didn't say anything to anyone but my family. They thought I should just wait and see, that I could be wrong about the killing close by. I don't like to tell the police about these visions because they just don't understand how it works. If it hasn't happened yet, there's nothing they can do anyway.

Two days later two women came up missing from the Baskin Robbins in Clarksville and I knew it had to be them. I hadn't gotten anything else on it, so I didn't have much to tell the police anyway. They found their bodies in a park in Clarksville not long after that. Their suspect's name was Reed, and he lived in Nashville Tennessee.

When I saw him on television, I knew they had the right man, but they didn't know what I did about him. I could pick up more killings he had committed. I knew he had been doing this for years but hadn't been caught. Now that they had him there was no need for me to get into it. It was over.

I think the worse vision that I ever had in my life came one morning while I was in school. The day was September the 10th 1991. The vision hit me so hard and so fast it took my breath away. Suddenly, I wanted to scream and run out of the classroom. I couldn't seem to get my breath, and my whole body just started shaking. My teacher gives the strangest look when I get up and rush out of the classroom. I didn't stop until I was out of the building. Then I stopped and took a deep breath. I didn't know what was happening to me, I just knew that I had to get out of there.

I felt like I had already made of fool of myself, and I didn't let go back to class. I thought would go down to a restaurant I knew of close by and have a cup of coffee. I thought maybe this would settle my nerves. Going in I set down in a booth and ordered coffee. The waitress brought coffee and I took a few sips, then a hit again. All I could feel was the urge to run. I felt like screaming, and telling everybody in the restaurant to get out, to run. I caught myself before I could do this thing

God. I would really have upset these people for no reason that I could have explained.

I went home because I didn't think I would be safe anywhere else until this passed. As I walked in the door, I could smell something burning. I can also hear what sounded like a bomb going off in my backyard. It seemed to shake the foundation of my house so badly that I had to grab the counter in the kitchen to hold myself up. I could see children and adults dying. I could hear children screaming and crying but couldn't make out what was going on. It looked like my kitchen was full of smoke so thick that I couldn't make out anything in the room. The whole house seemed to sway back and forth. I could hear rumbling sounds that reminded me of an earthquake.

I was so scared I didn't know what to do. It was so real I really thought we were having an earthquake, and the house was on fire. I started crying and trying to reach the back door. As I opened the back door, everything stopped.

It was a beautiful day; the sun was shining out in the backyard making it look so green. There was no evidence of a bomb going off or any other kind of disturbance. I glanced back over my shoulder into the kitchen, it was clear. There was no smoke, nothing. The shaking had stopped, and everything looked normal.

I sat on the back porch step and cried. I didn't know what to do, I was so scared. I had visions before that looked so real that I thought I was living them. They had never gotten to the point where everything around me shook and the room had filled with smoke. My body was shaking so hard I was scared to try and stand up. I sat there for more than an hour, trying to make since of what had just happened.

I couldn't get a look at anything around me while this was happening. I didn't know what to tell anyone because I didn't know what there was to tell. All I knew was that it was extremely bad. The worst vision I had ever felt, I knew a lot of people including children were going to die. I had no idea where it was going to happen or when. I just knew it was going to be the worst experience in what I thought then, in the history of Hopkinsville.

Finally, I made myself get up and go to the phone. I call the only person I could think of. By this time detective Lilies had retired from the police force. Now my contact is detective Scott Mayes. I called him but he was out of the office. I left message a describing what happened as best I could. I also told him about the children's screaming and crying and about all those people dying. I told him I didn't know where or when any of this would take place. I this knew that he needed to be ready for the worse thing that he could imagine.

After leaving the message I felt better. I knew that I would never feel settled until I found out what the vision had been trying to show me. I do that there was nothing more I could do than what I had just done. There was no one else to call. I had done the only thing I could.

The next morning, I was still thinking about it when the phone rang. It was detective Mayes telling me I had been right. I asked him what he was talking about. He said, "you don't know". I told him I didn't understand. He told me to turn on the television, that I would understand then.

I walked into the living room and switched the television on. Just like to rest of America I watched the Twin Towers in New York burn. I knew then that that was what my vision was trying to show me. It just wasn't clear enough at the time. I know deep in my heart that if it hadn't been clear, that no one would have believed me. `

I think this is what distinguishes the real psychics from the fakes. Most real psychics don't get into every case they hear about. Sometimes I know there are cases where you feel strongly about and feel the need to do something to help. I know I don't get into every case I pick up on; if I did, I would never have time for anything else in my life. I think most psychics will wait to be asked or wait to see if the police get anywhere before they contact them concerning what they have “seen”. I know from experience that this can be the hardest thing in the world to do.

The Unknown

This chapter covers a wide range of things that I have no answers to. I cover abilities that I don't understand or know how they work. I hope to help you understand them better from the way I describe them. I will tell you how they work with me and how I use them, as well as I can.

This is something I deal with every day of my life. My whole life in one way or another has dealt with this issue. Not only in my home life, but as someone who works with police departments and other agencies. I can say with all honesty that most of the time I have no idea what is going to happen to me from one day to the next. I have to wait just like everyone else to see tomorrow.

Most people tell me they really don't want to know what is going to happen in their lives. They feel that it should just come naturally. The people I talk to about being psychics tell me that knowing somehow would change their lives that it would make a difference in how they dealt with life and with people. I for one know this can be true, but I also know that sometimes it's better to know than be caught by surprise. The future is something everyone must deal with in his own way. It's not something you already know, but the part you don't know. It's something that even I wished I didn't know anything about sometimes. Seeing death or sickness and not being able to tell someone about it is very hard.

One of the ways I can see death in someone's future is they do not have a future. What I mean by this is that when I do readings and someone asks me about what will happen to them, I see a future up to a point then it stops, I know at this point they will have no future and are going to die. This is something that doesn't happen too often, but it has happened. At these times I tell the person that I can't read for him, because I don't see anything. I don't go into the part where they will die; I just stop reading.

Dealing with the unknown is something most people find hard to do, as in spirits, or ghosts as most people call them, because they are part of the unknown. They are afraid to talk about it in terms of life after death. They don't understand about life after death, so they are scared to get into it. This is unknown to them, and therefore not something talked about. They feel uneasy talking about it because they don't understand anything about it.

This could be because of the pain in their hearts from the loss of a loved one, or not being able to deal with the fact that there could be life after death, the fact that their loved one could be with them at that moment and not being able to see them is hard to grasp. Understanding that the two worlds are so close, and yet so far away is not easy to believe.

What most people connect with the unknown is what they see on television. What they are told is the unknown. Not knowing where to believe if this is possible. This to me is something I live with in my life in more than one aspect. I deal with what others feel is the unknown, and this is where I have a hard time dealing with other people outside my family and friends.

People are afraid of the unknown; not understanding this is as much a part of their lives is it is mine. They don't realize that every day they wake up, they are dealing with the unknown. Every time they get into a car and drive down the street they are going into the unknown. What I do is just take it one step further than they do. I go into this part of life knowing what is on the other side, dealing with it day by day, and knowing that there is a middle ground.

What I call the other side has been part of our history as far back as anyone can remember. The Indians believed in the spirit world, and that what we do in our everyday lives affect this world as well. The Greeks believed that there were Gods that held their lives in their hands, and that they did what the Greek Gods wanted. They believed that there were spirits that dealt with the unknown.

In our history there are periods in which people were burned at the stake because they were thought to be witches. These witches were thought of as people who deal with the unknown spirits and are able to rule others' lives by what they do. This is not the same thing as what I do, but in the mind of some it is the same. This goes back to not knowing what is going to happen in their lives. This is why psychics are thought of in some respects as witches, because do not understand what they do or how they do it.

There is a great deal of difference between a psychic and what people think of as witches. This is hard for some to understand this because they label them both together. This is because both deal with the unknown and are not understood. To explain this, isn't something that can be done in a day. There are those of us who can't explain why or how we know the things I have been asked if I believe in witchcraft. I don't know if I do or not. I have never had any dealing with it.

What makes it hardest for me is that people don't understand that I am like just they are, and that they could do what I do if they wanted to. This is something that they see as part of me and not something that could be part of themselves as well, and could be used for the better

There are parts to my life that I don't get into often, these are the things that I know no one will understand. There are times in my life that I wish I could wake up tomorrow and be like you, the woman and mother that people see every day, not the woman they have seen on television working a murder case or looking for someone that is missing.

The one ability I have that upsets a lot of people is the ability to hold something in my hand and tell you about the person who owned it. This is where most people stop and think about what I do, hard. They don't understand that when I pick up the same things, they do every day that I can't deal with it like they do. I must stop myself from opening up and reading everything I touch. This can be hard because I must keep alert for this. The things people take for granted in their everyday life is something I must watch out for. I can't just walk up to something and touch it. I must feel it out first, see what kind of vibes I get from it first.

One example I can relate to you is when I buy Tarot Cards. Most people can just walk up and pick up a box and read the label. I can't do this. I learned the hard way from getting my hand burned badly by a deck I just picked up that this could be dangerous for me.

While I was in Germany I stopped into the Stars and Stripes bookstore to look around. I saw they had just gotten a shipment of tarot cards in. I reached out and picked up the box to look at them and it felt as if I had grabbed a hot poker. The palm of my hand turned red and burned so badly thought I would cry right there in the store. A blister the size of a silver dollar came up in the palm of my hand from where I had been burned by the cards. I never understood how this could happen, just from picking them up. I did learn not to do it again though. Now I move my hand about an inch or two over them before touching them. If I pick up anything from them, I don't put my hands on them. I think this is because I'm sensitive to them. I had never had this happen to me before, but it taught me another good lesson. I don't just reach and grab something off the shelves now.

Another time that something similar happened to me was when a friend gave me a deck of Tarot cards that she had been given by her mother when she would younger. She had never used them and thought I would like to have them. I told her I would, and took the bag they were in. After I got home, I opened them and took them out. I could feel a tingling sensation go up my arm. The feeling you get when you touch an electric socket hit me. It didn't hurt much, but it surprised me. I dropped them very quickly. They scattered all over the floor. When the feeling was gone, I picked them up again, and understood why it was happening. They were one of the original decks of cards that had belonged to Alster Crewel. If you don't know who he is he, he's the one who started the satanic church. You could tell they were very old just from the way they looked. At the time I didn't know how old until a look on the computer to do some research. I knew the woman had originally come from England and her mother and grandparents were from there. This is how they came to possess this deck of cards.

If you know anything about tarot cards, you know that this man was the head of the Satanic Church and was known to be a very evil man. I don't know if I believe all I've heard about him, but I do know I didn't like what I read. I have been offered over ten thousand dollars for this deck, and I really don't know why I keep them, but I do. It's just not everyday someone gives you. a deck of tarot cards that belonged to this man. They are rare and may be worth a fortune, but I won't sell them.

I don't use them at all. I find that most of the time the pictures on them scare people. This is something I can understand. They are pictures of demons, and bad spirits. I read everything I could after getting them and didn't find anything I liked. I keep them always wrapped in black cloth. I don't bring them out unless asked to, which is never. The reason I don't use them is because I get strange readings with them. I pick up very bad things about people, and bad vibrations. This is something I can do without. Sometimes my family says that's the reason for my problems, but I tell them "I had them long before I got those cards."

I have lived with strange happenings all my life. I remember when I was small and stayed at my grandmother's. She raised a garden every year. Her garden looked like something you would see in a Southern Living magazine, green and lush with tomatoes as big as softballs. As I said before she was Indian and lived by a set of different rules than most of us. I remember one year we had a heat wave here in Kentucky. It was so hot that everybody's garden burnt up on the vines.

I remember following her around her garden while she chanted. I don't know what it was she said. At that time, I was really too young to understand that part of her life, I just knew when to watch and keep quiet. This was one of those times. She would walk around up one row and down the other chanting.

Whatever she was saying worked. That year she had one of the most beautiful gardens you have ever seen. While other people's gardens died, hers flourished. She would give other people food from her garden, and she seemed too always have enough. No matter who asked, she would give them lots of vegetables. She told me that some things were not meant to be understood, that it was just there in time of need. Now I wished I had learned what it was she had been saying, I would love to have the gardens she had. But I also know that it would be there to share with others, not just to keep for myself.

This is where the unknown comes into play in a lot of ways. How does this work? I don't know. I have never understood this or why she was able to do what she did. As far as the Tarot cards, this is something that I will probably never understand. How do they work? I know that mine feel as if they are a part of me. I can tell the minute someone puts their hands on them. I get a very strange feeling of something different when I pick them up. Is this something that other psychics deal with, or am I the only one? I have posed this question to other psychics and have yet to find a true answer.

There are other parts of my life that I find hard to understand. These are the feelings I get right before something bad happens. I know this happens to others, but why? I know this is something that not only psychics have to deal with, but normal people as well. Where do these feelings come from? Some say it's female intuition I don't know if it is or not, I just know it's there. I do think that it could come from the subconscious and is a way to warn us of what's to come.

I have learned that a lot of this comes from inside us all if we just listen. I can honestly say that my abilities are stronger than most other people I have asked. I have had them get to the point that I can't function. They cause me to cry for no reason, and I have had them to make me pass out. I have walked by people I don't know and feel the pain so strong that I have bent double. I know that we sometimes get these feelings about someone in our family, because these are the people we love. Most of us feel foolish when this happens and are afraid to speak up and warn others.

The one time this has happened to me that I couldn't deal with was when a friend of mine died. He was a very sweet person and we got along well. Others didn't seem to care for him because he was homeless. To me that was something I never really thought about. I saw him as a person, not being someone with money or a place to live. He would come to where I worked at the time and sit and talk to me. He would write poems and read them to me. I would sit and listen to him and wonder why he lived like he did. I knew he was a smart person, but I didn't ask. I knew if he wanted me to know he would tell me when he was ready.

I knew that that something was wrong when I got a pain in my chest and then as quickly as it came it was gone. I didn't know who had died; I just knew it was someone I cared about. That same afternoon I was told he had died of a heart attack. I knew then it had been him I had felt as he passed from one world into another.

I have been at the bedside of a person that has just passed away. I have felt the soul leave the body and know that at that moment there is a peaceful feeling that comes over the spirit of this person. I also know that in some cases I have picked up the goodbyes of these people to their loved ones.

Where do these unknown feelings come from? Some people call them intuition, I don't know if this is true or not. But I do know that they are a part of us and that we have no control over them. This is something we can't just shut off any time we want to. I wish this were true, but I know it will never happen.

I have grown mentally as well as spiritually in the last few years of my life. I have come to understand more about myself than I did as a young child or as a teenager. But even now I sometimes know that I need help with dealing with being a psychic. In the early years I knew that I didn't understand how it all worked and needed help. Now I turn to God for this help.

If I'm working on a murder case and I didn't seem to be getting everything I knew that I was of no use to them or me. I couldn't think straight most of the time because I felt I wasn't pulling my weight. I couldn't get into something as important as a murder case where someone else's life may hang in the balance. I didn't know where to turn.

I have always believed that my gift was a gift from God. that he had a reason for me being this way. I knew that I may not know what it was, but he did. So, this is where I turned. I asked him to help me deal with this gift in the way he saw fit. I also asked him for help in making what I saw clearer to me as well.

I know you don't make deals with God, but this time I didn't know what else to do. I prayed that he would make my visions clearer, and that if he was going to give this to me, not to give me just half of it. I knew there were other abilities that I had that I could use, but this one time it seemed important to go to the source.

I have always been told that he will answer your prayers in the way he sees fit, and this he did. He opened a whole new view of what was going on in the case I was working, He showed me things I would never have dreamed I could know. He has enhanced my abilities in ways that I never could have dreamed of. I feel that is why even to this day I find abilities I didn't know I had until a need them.

Once while I was married and living in Georgia, my family and I went fishing on the Chattahoochee River for the weekend we were camping for the weekend and had gotten everything set up and ready to start fishing. My husband and I sat there and watched as the sun came up. It looked like a beautiful day, and I knew it was going to be a great end to a hard week.

The children were playing close by where I could keep an eye on them. They had brought games along with them because they were too young to fish. They enjoyed the weekends at the river and had a good time while there. My oldest would sometimes bring a friend along because she was the only girl.

We sat on the riverbank for a while, and then I told my husband I wanted to go a little way down from where we were now. I could still see him and the children from where I was. The river inlet where we fished closed in at that point, and I wanted to fish from the inlet. The other bank was about twenty feet across from where I stood, and the water was shallower there.

I hadn't been standing there more than fifteen minutes when I looked up and saw a man standing on the other bank. He looked to be about fifty, but the thing that struck me most was he wasn't fishing. He was just standing there looking at me. I nodded my head at him and went fishing. I could see him out of the corner of my eye and knew he hadn't moved from the spot where I had first seen him.

He was wearing a vest like a lot of fishermen wear, the kind with a dozen pockets, and faded blue jeans. He wore a baseball cap, with some kind on writing on the front, but I could not read what it said. I didn't want to stare, but he never seemed to move. At first, I started getting nerves, but then I realized that something was different about him. He wasn't real.

I thought at first, I was imagining things, but when I took a closer look at him I knew I was right. To make sure I walked up the bank to see if he followed and he did. I started back to where my husband stood and told him about the man. He looked to see if he could see him and didn't. I knew this wasn't unusual, but I knew that there had to be reason he was there.

Finally, I told my husband that he needed to go call the police, because there was something the man wanted to show me, and I knew it couldn't be good. It had to be a body or something else that had to do with the man standing on the riverbank. I opened my mind and could hear him say. "Come with me." Then I knew I was right, he had to be a spirit. He turned away and started walking off in the other direction from me, I was still on the other side of the river but could keep up with him easily.

About fifty yards from where I had stood not more than twenty minutes ago, there was a body of a man floating in the water face down. The man I had seen was standing over the body pointing at it. I realized then what he was showing me. The body in the river was his body, and he was showing me where it was.

We called the police, and they came out to where we were. I showed them the body and told them I had just walked up on it. I didn't tell them about the man on the other side of the river or about him showing me where the body was. I knew that it would be impossible to explain to them how I had found it.

This is what I call the unknown, not because of what happened, but the thought that he knew I was there, and I could help him. Had he seen me before he died? I don't know, and probably never will. I do know that the little unanswered questions are the ones I find hard to deal with.

There are some things we will never understand. There are some things we aren't meant to understand. I firmly believe that we are not to know everything that there are some things beyond our understanding and always will be. We can ask the right questions and try to find the right answers. Who knows -maybe we will someday, but until then I'm happy not knowing.

The one thing that we all need to remember is that just because we can't touch it or may not be able to see it doesn't mean that it's not there. It's just not there for us to see at the time.

I do know that each of us have the ability to receive messages from the dead. To some it is a scary feeling to know that if you open your mind to the world around you, you will find there are unanswered questions out there.

One of the questions I have been asked by animal lovers is, do animals go to heaven. Well, I do know that I have seen the spirits of animals in places that I have lived in the past. I have seen them around people that I have read for. I believe that what I see is the spirit of these animals and I also believe that if they were put here by God then they are here for a reason just as we are.

I have seen theses and there have been other psychics who have as well. I have heard of animals coming back to check on these that are still alive. I have seen them in houses that I have been asked to come into to check for other spirits. I have seen them follow people around as if they were still alive. When asked about these spirits, people have told me that it was an animal they had loved and shared houses with for years.

As an animal lover I would like to believe this. I know that there are animals that have been in my life that I would love to see again when the time comes. I do know that I have never had any bad experience with animal spirits. I have come across them more than once and have not had anything bad happen to me when this happens.

The one thing I do know is that animals can pick up spirits long before we can. I have found that they are the best way of knowing that spirits are around us. I listen when my animals begin to act strangely. I have had my dogs pick up spirits around me before I do.

Another thing I'm asked about often is do I believe in evil spirits. The answer to that is YES! I do. I have had my share of meeting them. I know that I have found that mean people usually leave behind mean spirits, some to the point that I have felt like leaving wherever I was because the feeling of evil was so strong.

They are the same as we see on television, are not? Least the ones I have encountered, have made me sick, and have even hit me. As far as they go on television, no I haven't met this kind and hope never to do so. I'm not saying they are not out there. I'm saying that in my experience I haven't run into them.

One of the abilities I have that really surprises me is the ability for Remote Viewing. The reason I'm putting it in this chapter is because I don't understand this one at all. To me this is an unknown. I have never found anyone who can explain this to me.

I use this ability most when people come for readings. While I'm reading for them, I seem to get deep into their lives. I find myself seeing their home as someplace important to them and I can walk around. in them I can't turn around when I have "out of body experiences" so why now? This I don't know.

I can walk around in your house and see every little detail there. from the dishes sitting in the sink waiting to be washed to the curtains on the windows. I use this ability when I pick up a feeling of something bad happening at your home. I feel the need to look around until I find out what it is that is going to happen to you. I may see a fire in your kitchen or someone getting hurt because something was left on the floor.

I have been sitting talking to someone on business and been able to see his office on the other side of the country. I have found this ability comes in handy when I work on a case. I can see the person's house and most of the time see the inside of the killers. I find that this is handy because I can tell the police where to look for murder weapons.

I have heard of this being used for other reasons than what I use them for. It has been said the Government uses this to see what is going on in other countries. I know that I can cross-oceans. I know I can see what is happening in other countries, because I have done this to check on a friend whom I haven't heard from in a while.

I really don't like to do this, but I will say that I have in the past. Some might say this is a form of "out of body" and that I 'm just using it in another way. I know the difference by the way it feels. I know that I can feel my body and it's still where I left it. With "out of body" I don't have this feeling. There is not a feeling of just being there. I know that I can come back to my body anytime I feel the need to. With "out of body" I can't do this. I must wait until it's over.

This ability is still unknown to most, even to people who have studied it for years. How is this possible? I don't know; that is why I put it in the unknown. I do know it does have its uses.

Another of my abilities that is unknown to me is the ability I have to read minds. How I can do this, I really don't understand. I have had other psychics tell me it's just part of being psychic. I don't know if this is true or not. I really don't believe it is, because I've asked them if they can do it, and they said no. So, I'm back to square one.

I have a thing about privacy. I don't think that just because you can get into someone else's thoughts that you should. There are just some things that I or anyone else doesn't need to know. Sometimes it happens when I'm not even trying. I can walk by someone and pick up their thoughts. I don't ever say anything to them; I just go about my business and leave it alone. I figure if they wanted people to know they would tell us.

I have used it to have a little fun in class at school. My teacher really didn't believe in psychics and thought it was all a bunch of nothing. One day while he was talking about something or other, I took up the sentence where he stopped. I would answer him before he would ask the question. Finally, after class he asked me to stay behind, and tell him how I did it. I told him I didn't know it was just something that I could do whenever I wanted to.

He asked me what else I could do, and I told him. He asked for a reading then. After the reading I don't think he really knew what to do. There was no way I could have known the things I told him, and he knew it. I told him about things that happened when he was younger. I even told him what was coming for him in the future. When it came to pass, he told me I had been right. Now I don't think he disbelieves me now, but still doesn't understand how I did it.

Another thing that I have been asked about many times is angels. Are there really angels? I don't know if there are, but I do know that some of the things I've seen point to the fact. I have seen spirits that I knew were different from the usual ones I see. By this I mean that they put off a feeling of calm and peacefulness that I don't pick up from other spirits I've encountered.

One I remember very clearly was a spirit that put out a bright light when I saw her. She didn't have wings as most of us think of angels, but then I don't know if this is what I was seeing. The only way I can describe the feeling I picked up is goodness. I felt no fear at all while I was seeing her. With most spirits that I have picked up there is a feeling of caution that comes from past experiences. This one didn't make me even feel this. I just knew she was good, and that she wouldn't hurt me.

I picked her up at the home of a friend. Her child had just passed away, and I had stopped by to see her. I didn't know what I would pick up while I was there. I thought it would be the spirit of the child, but it wasn't. I knew that the child's spirit was in the house, but I didn't see her. There was only the spirit of a woman in the child's bedroom. Why she was there, I didn't know. I couldn't really say anything to her, because the child's mother was in the same room as me. It had only been a few days since her little girl had passed away. I didn't know how she would take this.

She never asked if her child was there, and I didn't feel that I should say anything until she did. I thought when the time came, she would ask me. I would wait until then before I said anything. Her child was what we know today as autistic, and she was the love of this mother's life. I knew she was hurting and would never recover from this loss.

The spirit of the woman I saw stood off in the corner of the child's room. She watched us as we walked around the little girl's room. She never moved from the spot where I first saw her. She also never tried to speak to me. Occasionally, I would glance over to see if she was still there, and she would be in the same spot each time.

I couldn't see through her as I do some spirits. I could tell she wasn't whole, but she wasn't misty either. It looked to me as if she was wearing a white gown of some kind that reached the tops of her feet. It looked as if she were wrapped in a white sheet. I really don't think that's what it was but that's what it looked like to me. I knew I had never seen a spirit like her before.

Also, I picked up a child and woman together not long ago. I knew there was something different about the woman. The child looked like other spirits I have seen. I have come across them in houses I have gone to check out, and I know what to look for with them. The woman seemed to glow, as did the one before. I felt that for some reason this woman was they're for the child, but I didn't know why.

This happened when someone asked me to check out some land for them, and I told them I would. I had been walking around for about fifteen minutes when I felt someone behind me. I first picked up the feeling that I wasn't alone, then a feeling that someone was watching me. When I glanced around me the first time, I didn't see anyone. I walked a little further and had this same feeling again, that I wasn't alone.

This time when I turned around, I first saw the child. She was standing about ten feet from me, looking at a house that had been built there recently. From her dress, I knew that she couldn't have come from the house. The dress she wore came just below her knees, but I still had the feeling that she wasn't from my time. I hadn't heard of anyone dying in the family that had just had the house built, and I knew that I would have been able to tell if she had come from the family.

Watching the little girl for a minute, I began to experience sadness. With this feeling came the first sight of the woman standing behind her. The woman was dressed in a light blue gown, with lace that reached her elbows. One minute I could see through her, then she would become solid. The woman never took her eyes off the little girl, never once moving away from her or going closer to her.

I waited for them to become more solid so I could open my mind and find out what I needed to know about them. Every time the woman became clearer, the less I could pick up the little girl. I don't know why this was, but I never had trouble opening up to them. For some reason I felt that the woman in blue was there to protect the little girl.

I decided to keep walking and come back later and see if they were still there. When I came back, I didn't see either one of them. Having seen them the first time, I knew that they were something special and that I might never see something like that again. Not just because they were there, but also because the woman gave off a sense of peace.

When people find out that I'm a psychic they ask me all kinds of questions One that I have been asked about often is reincarnation. I can only tell you what I know, and that is I feel that some do come back. Why? I don't know. Talking to people I have gotten many different answers. Some have told me yes, they do believe. Some say otherwise.

I think this is one unknown that may never be answered. I do know there is life after death, but is this the same thing? I have been told that we bring people from one life into another with us when we die, that we keep the same friends and family throughout each life. They just have different forms. The person in your last life who was your mother may now be your sister or the man you are married to in this one.

Two years ago, I went to a clinic that did hypnosis. I didn't know what I would find or what would happen. I knew that I was very sensitive to the spirit world and didn't know if they would be able to put me under. Or if he could I would come out of it easily. As I've said before I must watch what I do a lot of times. This was something I had wanted to do for years. but couldn't get up the nerve to do it.

After I arrived, I was led into a room the looked like an office. I was told to sit down in a chair across from the man who was going to hypnotize me. He explained that I would know what was always going on, and that I wasn't in any danger of not coming back. He didn't know how much I had wanted to hear that. I was still scared but wasn't going to back out after getting this far.

He dimmed the lights, but not enough so I couldn't see him or the room clearly. It was just enough that everything in the room was in the background. He told me to close my eyes and that he would lead me through this. He also told me that I had to keep one finger raised. I didn't know why and didn't think to ask at the time.

He told me to close my eyes and see a picture in my mind as he talked. He told me I was beside a small stream and that I could hear the water running over the rocks in the stream. That if I looked up, I could see a beautiful sky over head, and that I could feel a breeze as it touched my face. I could smell fresh air, coming in from all sides around me. And that I was to lie back and enjoy the smells and sounds around me. As I relaxed to this, I could feel my body relaxing into the chair.

Then he told me I would imagine a dark sky with a million stars in it. It was the most beautiful thing in the world. There was nothing around me but stars, they were so clear that it could see them twinkle. He said, "Imagine a golden staircase, and you standing at the top of this staircase". As I took each step down this staircase, I would be more relaxed. He would tell me to take another step then another. When I reached the bottom there would be an angel in purple waiting for me. He said that I should take her hand, and she would lead me up into the beautiful stars and that they would be all around me. As we reached a different set of stairs, I could hear his voice say that there is a big golden door and that I was to open the door and go through. He told me to reach and open the door so I could walk through. He said that on the other side of the door would be one of my past lives, and that I would see myself as someone else.

I remember reaching out and opening the door. As I took a step through the door, I could see daylight. I could feel a breeze on my face that felt warm and soft. I could see a man about the age of twenty standing on a large rock that stood some fifty feet in the air. To the left of him was a castle; it stood like a giant in the background. I could see the tops of the walls that surrounded the castle. It looked to be very old and had large holes in the walls close to the top edges. The sun shining on the castle walls made it give off a lot of heat, and I could feel it from where I stood.

I could tell that this man was myself, and it seemed like I knew his feelings, likes and dislike as well as I knew myself. He stood close to six feet. He didn't have a large frame, but very muscular shoulders and His hair came to rest on his shoulder and was a mixture of colors. I could see brown, and blonde alike. I could also see his eyes were a deep blue, and his skin was tanned by many hours in the sun. He had a full mouth with full lips that covered a chipped front tooth. It felt like I was standing by him but was also a part of him.

I could hear a voice that told me to look around me and remember everything I saw. To take in the sounds and smells that I picked up around me. I could also hear the voice telling me to look further back in my past. When I did, I could see a little boy with brown hair waving a stick. He and another little boy were having a sword fight. I could hear them both laughing and hear the sticks as they met. I knew this was myself I was seeing because the little boy had the same chipped front tooth as the man I had just seen. I could hear them talking but knew it wasn't English they were speaking. I didn't pinpoint the language, but I knew it was mine and that this was what I had spoken.

I could hear the voice again tell me to come back to where I had started from, and to look around at the people with me. The voice told me that the faces of the people around me would be those of strangers, but I would see the souls of these people. I would know them because I would also see the face I knew in this life.

The faces at first didn't register. I didn't know any of them, but as I looked closer, I could see people I knew. There was a woman standing close to me, dressed in a kind of robe. She was younger than I was, with black hair. Her face faded out and I could see my youngest son. I looked at the others and there were people I knew from years past. My oldest daughter's face covered the man who I knew as my father. My sister Polly was my mother. I could see others that went back all the way to my childhood.

Then I heard the voice telling me to open my eyes and come back to the room. I didn't want to come back for some reason I wanted to stay there with the people I was with. I could also hear the voice ask me what year it was and remember where I was at. I looked around again at the people that were there as they started to fade. I could feel myself being pulled back. That's the only way I can describe it, a pulling feeling. I felt no pain or any discomfort, but the thought of leaving made me feel sad.

The voice became clearer as I came back from wherever I had been. After a moment I opened my eyes and the man who had talked me through this was sitting across from me again. He sat for a minute and waited for me to realize where I was. He told me I went under very easily, and that at one point he thought I might have been under to deeply. He then told me why was to keep one finger up in the air. He said it was because if I went too deep my finger would lower. He told me when this happened, he would lift my finger and I would come back. He said that at one point that my finger didn't want to stay up and that he had to life it up and hole it to get me to come up.

When he asked me how I felt, I told him great, and that I had enjoyed it. He told me then that I could learn to do this myself and wouldn't need someone to help me. He asked me where I had been, and I told him. For some reason I knew I was in Scotland, and it was close to the fifteenth century. I don't know how I knew this; I just did. The time and place were as clear to me as if I had opened that door and come back here to my hometown just a lot earlier.

After leaving the clinic I thought about what happened. At first, I didn't know if it had been real or not. I didn't remember him telling me what to see or about the things I smelled in the air. I really think what made me believe it was that then I opened the golden door and stepped through. I wasn't a King or Queen of Scotland. I wasn't Elvis or the late Pope. I was just a guy like everyone else. I was nobody special. If it had been something that was put into my mind, why not be the King or Queen. Why not be someone famous like John Wayne or someone I admired. This is what really made me a believer.

He also told me that the next time I opened the golden door I might not be in the same place, that I might travel into another past life, and never come back to this one, that other people had traveled to as many as ten past lives and never been to the same place twice. Does this mean that we have more than one past life? I don't know. I do know that I want to try it again someday.

Is this the way to see past lives, and remember them? I can't say, but I do know that there is another side to the world we live in. I have seen it. Can both worlds meet in the middle or cross paths somewhere in the unknown? I think they might. I may never know. What I do know is that anything is possible. I have lived it.

One of the strangest abilities I have I didn't pick up until about two years ago. That was seeing "Auras". The first time this happened I thought the person was standing close to a blue light. It was the color of baby blue, very pale in color and not too strong. I didn't pay much attention to it and so I didn't say anything to anyone about it.

The next time it happened I saw a pink glow around the person's head and shoulders. We were outside in the day light, and I knew there wasn't anything pink that could be reflecting on to the man I was talking to. I glanced around behind him to see if I could tell where it was coming from. I didn't see anything there. This time I just watched it and took in what was happening.

I had heard of auras but had never seen one around anybody. I wondered why this man was pink and the last time the man's aura was blue. I didn't understand then that it has to do with what kind of energy you're putting out. Also, I didn't know that you put off different colors in sickness either. I was at a loss to understand what was happening and why. I knew that as I grew older, I developed different abilities. This one seemed to come out of nowhere.

Since then, I have noticed that very often I see auras around people. It's not like a halo or something to that effect. It doesn't surround just the head but the shoulders as well. It's a glow that seems to come out from the inside of the person. It doesn't twinkle or have rays shooting up from the body. It just seems to be there, as if it were part of them.

I have seen very dark gray and black auras. I have found that when I see these colors, it usually means death. I have come to associate red as the color people take off when they are very nervous. Pink and very light orange mean a very happy- go-lucky person. I also pick gray when someone has a medical problem that needs to be seen to. I pick up yellow around people who are confused about something in their life and don't know what to do about it. I have seen baby blues on people who are very much in love. I have also seen these same colors change quickly. I have also seen a white glow around spirits that I have seen, but not too many. These I account to angels and spirits that I feel are there for protection.

Others may see different colors for different things I only know what the colors I see tell me. This is energy you put off at times of stress or happiness. This is what I go by when I see auras. I have had them change from day to day, as the person's feelings change or as trouble comes. Is this something that anyone can do? I can't tell you that. I just know how I deal with these parts of my life, and how I understand them.

This chapter dealt with the unknown. Even to this day there are things I don't understand about others or myself around me. I do know that I have gotten used to strange experiences happening every day in my life. I don't think I really take them for granted, at least I hope not. I just urge you not to dismiss these strange and unusual things that happened to you. Don't try to explain away or think up a reason as to why these happen. Give yourself a chance to understand what is out there, and how it to be a part of your life. Always remember anything is possible with the human mind and spirit.

Psychics and Law Enforcement

In this chapter I want to give you a look at my experience working with the police. I also want to explain how I have worked with law enforcement, and how they work with me. I have worked with police departments, Sheriff's offices, FBI, CID, State Police in Tennessee, Kentucky, Georgia, and Indiana, TBI (Tennessee Bureau of Investigation), GBI (Georgia Bureau of Investigation) and Canadian Royal Mounted Police and in earlier years Interpol. Each has his/her own why of doing police work. As a psychic, most law enforcement officers don't know what to except. Those that have never worked with a psychic before only know what they have heard on television. Most are very hesitant about calling a psychic into work a case. They don't know what to expect in most instances because psychics use different methods to do their work. We may use ways that seem unnatural to them. And is most of the time considered unnatural by anyone's standards.

I want to say that working with a psychic isn't something one does every day, for law enforcement officers or the everyday person. I don't blame anyone for stepping back and taking another look at what I do and how I work. I know it's not easy accepting what I do as a normal way of life. Since starting college and majoring in law enforcement, I have learned a great deal about why they don't call a psychic unless they feel they have no other choice. The reason I chose the field of law enforcement for my degree was quite simple. I figured if I meet them about halfway and show that I understand to some degree how they work; they would be easier to except me and working with a psychic.

I have gotten to see the other side of their lives, not just the part I see while working with them. I have a new understanding of what law enforcement officers deal with within their everyday lives. They can be your best friends, or they can be your worst enemy, according to which wayside of the law you walk on. I have seen some of the things they go through while working on cases with them, and what I have learned from talking to them. I know that the job they have is a very hard one, and it isn't a picnic in the park dealing with criminals. It is a job I would never want to have to deal with every day. The reason I am taking law enforcement in college is that it helps me understand more of what they need from me as a psychic.

I do know that just from what I have seen, there is no way they can leave their work in the office. Dealing with murders and other criminals on a day-to-day basis is not an easy job, and what they leave behind in a day's work cannot be forgotten just because they close the door to their offices at night. There is just no way they can just walk away from it as if it never happened. I have seen bodies that were in such condition it was hard to believe that once upon a time they had been human. I have seen children and adults as well that have been beaten to death by those that claim to have loved them. I get called into most cases after the body has been taken away, and I don't have to see it firsthand. Seeing it in my mind or in a vision is hard enough. Having to deal with this in their jobs almost every day takes its toll on them.

I go into a case not wanting to know anything about the victim, or the person they think might have done the killing. Most police officers don't understand why this reasoning. I have been asked, "How can you work a case without knowing anything about it?" I try to explain to them that I don't want to know anything because I don't want it to influence my mind about a case. I want to be clear headed and know what I see is a vision and not something they told me about.

Police officers deal in facts and clues to solve a case. This is how they find criminals, and after working with me they come to understand that I'm not lucky enough to work with facts. What I see could be a picture of a killer, or what has happened to the victim before their death. I may start out getting an image of the victim as a child and carry it on into the present. I may pick up on the killer's life and must go from there, working my way backwards. As I said before, it can be like a puzzle that I have to put together. This sometimes doesn't come in an instant but may take hours or days. I sometimes may not get anything at all. Usually, I'll know not long after I start talking to them about the victim that I will not be able to pick up the victim or the killer.

I always tell the police officer that I may not be able to help you. I never tell them I can if I can't. This is not how I work if I can't help them, I would just be wasting my time and there's, I don't believe in getting anyone's hopes up just to let them down. This is not the way to get a good reputation as a psychic.

I have had police officers ask me questions about themselves, just to see if I was any good and could answer them. I try to answer them in a way that they will find comfortable. I don't go into big details about their lives, although I could. I just answer the questions they ask. I have found that it's not only the younger officers that are willing to use psychics. I have worked with officers that are in their late fifties and early sixties. I have found that open minds in the field of the unknown are what count. I have found that it depends on if they have had a bad experience with a psychic in the past, Psychics are the same as anyone else; there are good and bad. In all ranks you cannot judge us all by one psychic with whom you have had a bad experience.

Police work is known to be one job that carries a lot of stress, and it is also known that it carries a high mortality rate. Suicide is high among police officers, and even harder on their families. This has been proven in police departments all over the world. As a psychic I can relate to some of what they go through. I have had to deal with this stress of working with death. I know that after a big case, I must hold back on working on another case for a while because of the stress from the last case. This is because my job is not only physical, but mental as well.

With police officers I have worked with, most tend to step back and watch how I work, watching as I go through the readings and trying to get a good hold on what it is I'm picking up. They ask how I do this and how I get this information. I try to tell them by giving examples. Law enforcement officers are not used to someone coming in on a case and knowing what is going on before they are told. I know it's hard for them to open up about a case, but they soon realize that it doesn't matter one way or the other. I will know about the case without their saying a word. Any good psychic can tell the officers, not wait to be told the facts beforehand. We know by pictures in our mind or by feelings we get, not by words.

One part that most law enforcement officers have a hard time understanding is how I know what I do. I don't even need to know the name of the victim or the description. Most of the time I just ask for a picture and go from there. I sit down and let my mind open to that person and feel the energy he/she has left behind. Sometimes this doesn't work, and I ask what the officers need to know, because I'm not getting anything from the picture or personal article of clothing or item of the victim that they have given me. This doesn't happen often; I don't usually have trouble picking up anything this way, but it has happened.

Psychics will never replace the law enforcement officers that work in these cases. Psychics are there to help solve a case, not to take it over. I have found that some departments feel that if a psychic is there they will try to take over, or that they can't help them. I have worked with law enforcement agents that have changed their minds after they see how I work. This is because they began to understand how I work.

They feel that they understand what is happening before I'm through. I try my best to help them understand how and what I do as I go along. I don't try to keep them in the dark about how I work. I will try to explain what I'm doing as I work. That way, it doesn't leave them out.

There is one thing I would like to tell law enforcement officers. When you do call in a psychic, make sure she or he can give you the names and numbers of agencies they have worked with in the past. If not, then think about it before you use this person. Any psychic that is any good will have names and numbers of references to give you. If by some chance a psychic calls in on a case she or he has seen or heard about, be it television or newspaper, ask for names so you can call about references; any good psychic will volunteer this information. If you have the chance to ask people the psychic has read for, ask! You may not get details, but you will know if she or he is real or one thing that law enforcement officers need to understand about working with a psychic is, the difference in techniques. Not all psychics work the same way. Each may have their own method of working a case.

A lot of what we deal with is what law enforcement calls "gut feeling". Psychics have gotten to the point where we know how and when to listen to this feeling. Some of us also see pictures in our mind about what is going on in the victim's lives. It may not make any sense to you at the time, but it usually comes up somewhere later in the investigation.

Most psychics keep notes as they go along, others may leave it to the officer in charge of the case to do this. I do both this way I can go back and look over it and try to keep up with what is going on. I try to make sure that the officer I'm working with is kept up to date on anything I pick up. Whatever it may be, I make sure they have even the least little detail of anything I find. I know that it could be what breaks the case.

I will tell you that not all of what I find makes sense to me either. I find it hard sometimes to explain what I do see. Not knowing the families or the victim makes it that way. I try to start with just what I pick up at the beginning, and then go from there. Later, after I have gotten all, I can from the picture, I then open my mind up to anything that wants to come through, and I write it down. I do this best after the day is over, and I get to slow my mind down.

When I work with law enforcement officer looking for a killer, at the end of the day I try to rest, but sometimes it doesn't work that way. I may be resting body wise, but my mind is still on the case I'm working. I find that I even pick up bits and pieces while sleeping. I keep a notepad beside the bed to write down what I pick up in the night. I don't want to miss anything that might help find a victim or a killer if I can help it. When I 'm working a case, I start about eight or nine in the morning and work until about four or five that afternoon. By the time night comes around I'm wired and can't sleep.

I find that going to the scene of the crime helps, so if you're working with a psychic, she or he may ask to do this. I have found that when someone is killed, he leaves what I call an energy field behind. This I can pick up at the scene where the body is found and can pick up more vibrations from where the killing took place. I may even be able to see the murder as it happened in an image I get in my mind. I have done this while the body is still there. I won't say that I like being there. I just know that I have picked up the victim as he died and have "seen" a good picture of the person who did the killing. This doesn't happen often (being at the scene of the crime while the body is there) and I wouldn't advise anyone, if you don't have to be there, don't be.

One thing that I use to help when finding a body is a pendulum. I use this to break down an area on a map in which to start looking. This way, time is not spent on going over an area where the body is not. I start out with a cross draw on the map, one line down the middle of the map and one line across the center. I hold the pendulum in the middle where the lines meet and ask where the body is from this point. Whichever way it goes, I break this area down again until I can pinpoint where I think the body is. Most law-enforcement officers wonder how something on the end of a chain can find a body. How it knows where to look. I really don't know the answer to this, only what I've read. I do know that I have found bodies this way and have found it to be accurate and a lot of cases. I do know you just can't pick up pendulum and expect one to work. You hold them in your hand, and what some call playing with it. This way it picks up the vibrations and energy from your body and can distinguish you from anyone else who touches it.

Once the pendulum knows you and you know what it's showing you, it's easy. I have had law enforcement officers ask me questions while I was using the pendulum and I have given them the answers it gives me. The question must be asked in a yes or no manner. This way the instrument can answer you.

This works the same way one finds water by "dowsing" It looks for the energy of the person you are asking about.

I feel that most law enforcement officers are willing to take help anyway they can get when they are up against a wall. They are willing to try something they know nothing about just to solve a case. To those I say thank you. Officers that are open to the idea of psychics make it easier for both of us.

What most law enforcement officers don't understand is that we may have ways of going about it that will be strange to them. At some point it may seem to them that we are not doing what we are there for, but with most psychics, when we get into a case, we have vision after vision, and we have to work this out in our own minds first. It asked me to make some since to us first before we can even start to try and explain it to them. We may see the victim with a person but not get a good look at them or what is going on until it's time to. We may get pieces of a vision, or too much to process at one time. It's like a puzzle; we must try and put it together before we can go any further.

Sometimes I don't like to say anything about something I see, because it's so unnerving to me. I may pick up a person that the victim had words with in the last few days and mistake it for the time of death. This is why some psychics get a funny look on their face when this happens. They are trying to make heads or tails of what they are seeing. The visions they are seeing have to play out for them to really know what's happening. They may sit looking off into space, or just sit with their eyes closed. This is something that each psychic has to do that works for him or her in a given situation.

The most important thing I can say about being a psychic is that if given a chance we can help in an investigation. We may be able to fill in the gaps that are missing in a case, parts that are missing from the view of the normal person. We may also be able to help in finding people that are missing. I have been asked about someone who is missing only to pick up that just wants to be left alone. The hardest part is trying to get the law enforcement officer to understand what it is I'm picking up. If I don't get a full vision, it's hard to explain to them that I do see.

The next time you feel you are at the end of an investigation and need help or you hit a wall; don't hesitate to call upon a psychic to help. I feel that is why we have this ability, to help when the time comes. Call around and ask other departments if they know of a psychic that can help. If so, make sure she or he can do what it is you need to do. There are some that have abilities that others don't have. The one thing to remember is we are not alike. We do not all work the same way, and if given a chance we can make a difference.

I do not use my talent to make money from the police department. Here in Hopkinsville where I live, I don't charge the police department. I'm trying to give back a little of what I have been given. This is my home and my friends. I may have to call on them someday and I can feel now that I have given a part of me that others can't give.

Edgar Cayce

The reason I am putting a short chapter in my book about Edgar Cayce, is not only do I have and use some of the same abilities that he had, but he was known as a great man. He was known as the Sleeping Prophet. Edgar Cayce was born on a farm outside my hometown of Hopkinsville, Kentucky. He lived most of his life here and is now buried here in Riverside Cemetery.

Edgar Cayce was known for his ability to leave his body and travel to other parts of the world to diagnose people that wrote to him for help. By leaving his body, I mean his mind or spirit would leave his human body. He would go into a self-induced trance and seek out those in need of his help. He was also known to have used medical techniques that were way beyond his time. He was known to prescribe medicines that would not have otherwise been used for that proposal. He was known to describe how to make medicine that had never been heard of at that time.

As I have said before in this book, I am clairvoyant and clairaudient, and can see and speak to the dead. While Edgar Cayce died January 3,1945, I have looked to him for advice, in my time of need, when I was unable to work a case for one reason or another. I would go to his grave site and ask him for help. This is not something I have done with any other person alive or dead.

I did this on a very important murder case that happened here in Hopkinsville. I didn't know if I could reach him, but I knew there was no one else I could turn to, no one that would know what I was going through and understand. I was at the crossroads of my life and didn't know if I should get into the case. I had my family, but not being psychic, they could only tell me that I had to do what I could to help. I knew this wasn't the answer I needed to hear. I needed to know if it was right, not what everyone thought I should do.

I had heard of Edgar Cayce, because here in Hopkinsville he was and is a well-known figure. His family still lives and works here. I had never read a book about him or been to any function they gave about him. To me he was just the Sleeping Prophet, a person who had passed away long before I was born.

The murder case I was working was driving me crazy I was getting to the point I had to make a discussion. I couldn't keep putting it off any longer. I had turned to God to ask him help, and I really knew I didn't need anyone's help but his. It was driving me crazy not knowing what to do. A murder case is not something you just jump in to; it is something that affects the lives of everyone involved. So, you must think about more than yourself. You must think of those in the family whose case you're working on, and your own family also.

I told my sister I would be back, and I drove around town for a while. I found myself turning into Riverside Cemetery where Mr. Cayce is buried. I had no idea why I was there, or what I was going to do. I had no idea where in the cemetery he was buried and had to stop someone and ask. They pointed out his grave and I walked over to it. I was really surprised by what I found.

I was looking for a large gravestone, one that would have befitted this man I had heard so much about. This is not what I found. What I did find was a very small stone about eight by eleven. There were no signs stating here lay Edgar Cayce, there was nothing surrounding him but those he had loved in life.

It was a beautiful day, and the sun was shining. I could see others walking around the cemetery visiting family grave sites and looking for others they might have known while alive. There was nothing around his gravestone to sit on, so I knelt on the edge of his stone. I told him who I was and why I was there. That I needed his help in deciding about what to do. I really didn't think that I would be able to make contact, but I was wrong.

I waited for a moment and then I felt a breeze blowing that seemed to come from nowhere. There was a warmth about it that made me feel that I was doing the right thing by being there and that I would get the answers I felt I needed.

‘ I hadn’t been there more than five minutes when it seemed to turn dark all around me. I couldn’t see the other people in the cemetery any longer. I couldn’t even see the man who not more than ten minutes before had shown me the way. I didn’t feel any fear, nor did I feel that I was in danger.

A moment later the sky cleared and there on a bench sat a man I had never seen before. He sat with his legs crossed, with one arm over the back of the bench and the other on the arm of the bench. He was dressed in a brown suit and white shirt. On his head sat a hat of brown about the color of his suit.

He looked at me and waited for me to speak. I didn’t know who this man was, but I did know he could help me. I felt this inside my being and knew that feeling and what it meant. I said “hello” and he nodded his head. Then I told him why I was there. That I didn’t know what to do. I needed answers to go on. He sat still and stared at me, as if to make sure I was telling him the truth.

Finally, he spoke. He said “No one can answer your questions but yourself. You have to be able to live with yourself, knowing that what you are doing is right. If you can do that, then yes, you are doing what is right. If not, then you should listen to your heart, and let it guide you. “I knew then that this man who had shared with me his thoughts was Edgar Cayce. He had heard me and knew that I needed his advice.

I waited to see if he had anything else to say, but he didn't. I could feel that same breeze coming from nowhere again. I glanced up to the sky and back to where he had been sitting. He was gone, as was the bench he had sat on. I could now see the people walking around again. Over to my right there was the man who had shown me the grave site.

I sat thinking about what he had said to me. He had told me the same things I had been thinking myself. I knew that being able to live with yourself is what you really must think about. If you don't think you can live with something, don't do it. It may come back to haunt you later.

I left there not knowing where else I needed to go. What he had said to me played repeatedly in my mind, until I was sure I understood what he was saying. I knew that if anyone knew how I felt it was him. Not only because of who he was, but because in his day it was hard for him to be the man he was and to do what he felt was right.

In his time Edgar Cayce was a strong believer in God and believed that God's way was the right way. I also knew that people still believed this could be the devil's work. I knew he had to prove himself before he would be believed.

The second time I visited Edgar Cayce's grave was when I was going through a bad time with myself. I knew that I couldn't change what or how I was, that I had been born this way for a reason. As I've said before I may not understand it, but God has a reason why he wants me like this. I know that I am here for a reason.

This time he told me that what is "God's will" will be done, and there is nothing we can do to change it. He said he believed that God had a purpose for me. He also told me not to fight what I had, that if I could help those in need, then that is what I should do.

I have been to numerous churches here in town. I t seem to me that everything would be all right until someone found out about my psychic abilities. Then things would change. I wouldn't be treated the same after that. I have even had my children told in church that I was in with the devil. And that I was evil. This was when I stopped going to church altogether. I know in my heart that God knows that what I am doing is what he wants me to, not what someone else wants. I know that in Edgar Cayce's time it had to be just as hard on him as it is for me.

Later on in Edgar Cayce's life he moved to Virginia Beach, Virginia, where he founded the Association for Research and Enlightenment. His readings are kept there to preserve his work for everyone to use. It is also a school of learning where one can go to get a degree in this field. Numerous books have been written about him and his family, and what he had to go through. There are also other areas of Edgar Cayce's life took him as well. At the ARE in Virginia Beach, there are numerous other areas of psychic phenomena involving him, such as ESP, and Past Lives.

I am not saying that my ability to look inside the human body will ever compare to Edgar Cayce's I don't think it does or ever will. I do know that I have heard of few , if any, who can do this, at least not in the same way I do. Cayce's gift goes far beyond mine and I will admit I'm glad that I don't have to live with it. Not that I wouldn't try to help others in the same way he did, if it ever does. My ability to look inside your body doesn't stop at just what I see. It may show me something that you could do to help yourself. I can not go as far as he did, because in this day and time it is against the law to do this.

Edgar Cayce died January 3, 1947, leaving us with a lot of unanswered questions, some that may never be answered, and others that may be answered in the future. There is one thing that I do know. If there is such thing as reincarnation as he believed, then I hope to one day meet this man and understand the "why's" that go unanswered for me.

Search and Rescue

At some time or another everyone has heard about search and rescue dogs. I had the chance to work with them and found them fascinating. I had raised dogs most of my life, but never had had any reason to meet this type of dog. Like you I had heard of them, but only knew what I had learned from television and the newspaper. While I was working on the case of the missing soldier at Fort Campbell, these dogs were brought in to go over the location I found. I was lucky enough to be able to work with handlers and the dogs as well. I came to respect both for what they do, and how they do it. I also was able to follow along with them as they searched for the body. I learned of the search and rescue dogs from a friend of mine. He told me that there was a couple in Cadiz, Kentucky that had just such dogs. I called and talked to Carrie Lynn and Jim Gray about having them bring their dogs in on the case. Also, I was able to talk to Reta Tinsley the founder of the Stewart Co. Search and Rescue in Dover, Tennessee. Talking to The Grays, I found that they have worked their dogs in many different parts of the country and have had a good successes rate in finding missing persons. They raise search and rescue dogs in their home and have trained with others in different parts of the country as well. I found that there was more than one kind of search and rescue dog. Not only are they able to hunt on land but also in the water. Carrie Lynn and Jim Gray raise what is known as air scent and ground scent dogs. Carrie Lynn described to me how they train these dogs. They related to me what they look for in a dog and how they go about this training.

They start with a puppy about the age of six to eight weeks of age. They look for a dog that is nosy and that isn't shy. It must show some submissiveness but not too much and must like people. They also look for a dog with stamina. Carrie Lynn told me that she prefers a German Shepherd for air scenting and Blood Hound for tracking.

They start the puppy out playing games at about the age of ten weeks old. They use hot dogs as a way of doing this. By breaking off pieces and smashing them into the dirt with your foot. They do this along a path to get the puppy used to tracking a scent. This also breaks off grass and leaves the scent of the person that has just walked down the path. As the puppy follows the scent of the hot-dogs, he finds the person who left the scent. Someone other than the person who has left the scent walks with the puppy down the trail, until they come upon the person. When this happens, they give the dog a treat to show it did a good job and this was the way to earn treats. In about two weeks, they send the puppy down the trail alone. They start with short easy games such as hide and go seek, not putting much distance between the person and the puppy so that they will be easy to find. he starts upwind of the puppy so the sent will come back to the puppy. One of the most important things about the training is everything is positive. They make the training a game the puppy will play willingly. Carrie also told me she used tennis balls with the scent of a cadaver on them to play with. This lets them become familiar with that smell in disturbed ground. The trainer didn't let the dog dig at the spot because it could have been a crime scene.

The next day Jim Gray and another trainer went back to the area where we had been the day before. Jim took another dog around the area to see if this one would make the same hit. It did. Not only did his second dog make the hit; the other trainer's dog did as well. The hits were reported to the police that day and then their job was over. It's up to officials to go from there.

While talking to Reta Tinsely, I learned also that dogs of this kind have been known to find bodies in up to two hundred feet of water. In her experience she has had her dogs find bodies in thirty feet of water. One such case was in Cypress Bay, just off the Tennessee River. The victim drowned at about five thirty-one evening. The search and rescue dogs were called in at about nine o'clock, and the dogs found the body by nine-thirty that same night.

Dogs that hunt for bodies in water start out at about the same age. as other search dogs. These dogs start off at the shoreline in shallow water with a piece of cadaver on a string.

Then the trainer walks the dogs from downwind. This way the wind brings the scent back to the dogs. Later divers are sent into the water and then the dogs are taken in a boat over the divers until the dog picks them up. When they find the divers, the divers are brought out of the water, and they give the dogs praise. Mrs. Tinsely told me she uses about a two- inch piece of cadaver to work with. In deep water Mrs. Tinsely uses a cricket tube. This is sent down into the water to depths of thirty feet, as the dogs become more familiar with what they are looking for.

I also learned that the body sheds forty thousand dead cells a minute. These cells float to the top of the water, this is what the dog picks up on when taken out in a boat. At one point Mrs. Tinsley told me about a body that was covered in a wet suit. The only part that was exposed was the face. The cells from only this part of the body were enough to find the drowned victim.

These dogs have a hard time working in very hot and cold weather. In hot weather there is usually not enough wind moving for them to pick up the scent. In cold weather there are similar problems. It is best to work with these dogs on hilltops and ridges in the early morning. and in hollows in the late evening. This is when there are better weather conditions in which to work.

I am happy to say it was great to work with Carrie Lynn and her husband Jim. I have been asked to come out and watch them as they run their dogs through their training, and even training a dog myself. I can hardly wait until then. I was even told I could bring one of my own dogs out there and see if it has what it takes to become a cadaver dog.

GLOSSARY

Here are some of my abilities and their meanings.

AURA'S--A colored energy seen around people.

CLAIRVOYANTS--The ability to see the spirits of people that have passed away.

CLAIRAUDIENCE--The ability to talk with spirits.

DOWSING-- To use a pendulum to find people that are missing or murdered.

ESP-- This is the ability to read other people's thoughts.

OBE--Out of Body Experience-- The ability for the spirit to leave my body.

MEDIUM-- The ability to call spirits.

PRECOGNITION-- The ability to see and tell of the future.

PSYCHOMETY--The ability to know the history of something from touch.

REMOTE VIEWING-- The ability to see something thousands of miles away.

RETROCONITION-- The ability to see into someone's past.

TELEPATHY-- The ability to read minds.

There are other abilities that I have but that are not explicitly defined.

Made in the USA
Columbia, SC
01 May 2025